The Unofficial
COLTS
Trivia Book

Dale Ratermann
with H.W. Kondras

Blue River Press
Indianapolis, Indiana

Cover designed by Phil Velikan

Editorial Assistance provided by Dorothy Chambers

Printed in the United States of America

10 9 8 7 6 5 4 3 2 1

Published by Blue River Press

Distributed by Cardinal Publishers Group

2222 Hillside Avenue, Suite 100

Indianapolis, Indiana 46218

www.cardinalpub.com

Table of Contents

Chapter 1
History

Can you imagine Peyton Manning playing in Yankees pinstripes or in the shadow of the famed Green Monster of Boston's Fenway Park? Maybe not, but a look at the Colts' family tree, and that's not far from the truth.

The team has been the Indianapolis Colts since 1984 when Bob Irsay packed up the moving vans and fled Baltimore in the middle of the night. From 1953-83, they were the Baltimore Colts. However, the team that became the Baltimore Colts in 1953 was the relocated Dallas Texans, which themselves were the relocated New York Yanks of 1950-51 that called Yankee Stadium home. Before that, they were the New York Bulldogs, playing in the Polo Grounds in 1949. Fenway Park was the team's home from 1944-48, when they were the Boston Yanks (founded by Ted Collins and singer Kate Smith).

Confused? Let's add a limb to that family tree. The original Baltimore Colts were not even part of the National Football League. They were founded in 1946 when the bankrupt Miami Seahawks of the All-America Football Conference were moved to Baltimore and renamed the Colts. Following the 1949 season, the National Football League and the AAFC merged, and the Colts were assigned to the NFL for the 1950 season. But after a 1-11 record, the original Colts disbanded. In 1952 the league spearheaded a ticket drive to return a team to Baltimore. The drive succeeded; the franchise sold 15,000 season tickets in six weeks and were awarded the Dallas Texans franchise that began play as the new Baltimore Colts in 1953.

No wonder Mayflower's moving company stayed in business so long.

History Questions

1. Who is credited with naming the team "Colts?"

2. Where did the new Colts in 1953 come from?

3. What were the colors of the original Baltimore Colts?

4. When did the Colts start wearing blue and white?

5. What was the name of the league the first Colts team played in?

6. Which team was purchased and moved by a group from Baltimore in 1946 to begin the Colts franchise?

7. When was the Colts' first season in the NFL?

8. After the original Baltimore Colts were dissolved in 1951, who was the principal owner of the new Colts in 1953?

9. In one of the biggest trades in pro-sports history, how many players were involved in a 1953 Colts-Browns deal that included Don Shula?

10. In which season did the Colts begin wearing face masks?

11. The Colts have played just one game that drew a 100,000+ crowd. Where was that game played?

12. When were horseshoes first placed on the sides of the Colts' helmets?

13. In 1969, three NFL teams were moved to the American Football Conference. Which teams joined the Colts in the move?

14. What happened minutes after the Colts' home playoff loss to Pittsburgh in 1976?

15. When was the first NFL players' strike that resulted in a loss of seven games on the Colts' schedule?

16. When the Colts moved to Indianapolis in 1984, which moving company transported the team's equipment to Indy?

17. When was the Colts' only winless season?

18. Which team did the Colts tie that season?

19. Who was the starting quarterback that season?

20. When was the second NFL players' strike that caused the cancellation of games?

21. Who did the Colts play in the first playoff game in Indianapolis, following the 1999 season?

22. Who was the first person enshrined in the Colts' "Ring of Honor"?

23. What is the Colts record for most consecutive wins?

24. What is the Colts record for most consecutive losses?

25. What is the Colts record for most points scored in a game?

26. In which season did the Colts last record a shutout?

27. Who had more in their Colts career:

    Rushing yards – Eric Dickerson or Marshall Faulk?

    Pass receptions – Bill Brooks or John Mackey?

    Passing yards – Jack Trudeau or Bert Jones?

    Interceptions – Eugene Daniel or Mike Curtis?

    Punts – Chris Gardocki or Rohn Stark?

    Touchdowns – Marvin Harrison or Lenny Moore?

    Field goals – Dean Biasucci or Cary Blanchard?

    Points – Lou Michaels or Edgerrin James?

28. In which country did the Colts open their 2005 preseason schedule?

29. Besides the Hoosier/RCA Dome, what is the only stadium in Indiana to host a Colts pre-season game?

30. From 1999-2006, the Colts had the best regular-

season record in the NFL. Which team was
second, six wins behind?

31. Name the four stadiums the Colts have played
in on the road versus the New York Giants.

32. Which of these players appeared in a playoff
game for the Colts: Art Schlichter, Marshall
Faulk, Lenny Moore, Matt Bouza, Eric
Dickerson, Lamont Warren, Chris Hinton, Ken
Dilger, Adam Meadows or Sean Dawkins?

33. Who is the Colts' current, longtime radio
announcer?

34. Entering the 2007 season, what was the year
and who was the opponent in the Colts' last
overtime game?

35. What is the name of the new Colts stadium that
will open in 2008?

36. Was the Colts single-game attendance record
of 61,479 set in Baltimore or Indianapolis?

37. What was the name of the Colts stadium in
Baltimore?

Answers on pages 100-102

Colts History

```
B U Y T S H U L A Q T S Q G K
Z L N R S H W P D V U D Y Z B
L S H I R R E W O L F Y A M S
Z H I T T E H C R A M F I H U
D E Y L R A B M B R E K R A P
V R N O O K S O I E D L S A E
X O O A P P O H H M S D A M R
X M S S S A A M C A K D Y W B
C I I G E A D N R N U S T P O
C T R D O N O V A N L T U C W
J L R R U T B B M I S X W B L
T A A H H U W L F N D Y M D X
Q B H Z J E G S O G V N O G L
H P I S U P E R B O W L I I I
T D K Z E J T Q X G M F Z Y Q
```

Baltimore
Berry
Donovan
Ewbank
Harrison
Indianapolis
Irsay
Manning
Marchetti

Marchibroda
Mayflower
Moore
Parker
Rosenbloom
Shula
Super Bowl III
Super Bowl XLI
Unitas

Answers on page 102

Chapter 2
Championships

While Super Bowl XLI may seem like the most exciting game the Colts have ever played, the team has played several of even more historical significance. The franchise can claim three Super Bowl appearances (including two wins) as well as three NFL Championship game appearances (including two wins). The Colts played in two of the NFL's most memorable games ever. The 1958 NFL Championship Game has been called The Greatest Game Ever Played. The Colts were also in Super Bowl III, when Jets quarterback Joe Namath guaranteed a Colts defeat and then led the AFL to its first Super Bowl victory.

1958 NFL Championship Game

This contest was dubbed The Greatest Game Ever Played for a reason. The Colts had lost to the New York Giants by just three points earlier in the season. The two teams met again in the title game on December 28, at Yankee Stadium. In one of the first nationally televised games, quarterback Johnny Unitas directed the Colts to a 14-3 halftime lead. The Giants dominated the third quarter and went ahead early in the fourth on a 15-yard touchdown pass. Trailing 17-14 with two minutes remaining, the Colts drove 90 yards for a field goal, tying the game with seven seconds left.

Since there had never been an overtime game in NFL history, most of the players thought there was no winner. "When the game ended in a tie, we were standing on the sidelines waiting to see what came next," Unitas said. "All of a sudden, the officials came over and said, 'Send the captain out. We're going to flip a coin to see who will receive.' That was the first we heard of the overtime period."

But it wasn't the last the world would hear of overtime. The Giants had the ball first but could not score. Then Unitas took the Colts 80 yards in 13 plays, the last one a one-yard touchdown run by Alan Ameche to give the Colts a 23-17 win and their first NFL title.

1958 Trivia

1. Running back Alan Ameche rushed for 65 yards and two touchdowns. Who was his running mate who ran for 30 yards on 11 carries?

2. Who was the Colts kicker who atoned for missing 27- and 46-yard field goal attempts by booting the game-tying 20-yarder in the final seconds of regulation?

3. Who was the Giants leading rusher with 60 yards on 12 carries? (Hint: He went on to a highly successful broadcasting career.)

4. Who was the Colts punter who averaged 50.8 yards on his four punts?

5. Which Colts receiver caught a championship game-record 12 passes for 178 yards and a touchdown?

1959 NFL Championship Game

So we meet again – Colts versus Giants in the NFL title game. Baltimore Colts fans might consider this the Second Greatest Game Ever Played. The Giants led 9-7 after three quarters, but the Colts intercepted three passes in the fourth to rocket them to a 31-16 win in Baltimore. The only championship game played in Baltimore, this contest featured many of the same stars as in the previous year – Johnny Unitas, Alan Ameche, Raymond Berry, Frank Gifford, Pat Summerall and Sam Huff.

1959 Trivia

6. The Colts intercepted three passes in the final quarter. Which defensive back had two of those and returned one 42 yards for a touchdown?

7. The Giants got on the scoreboard first with a field goal by kicker Pat Summerall. How did he get the nickname "Pat"?

8. Where was the game played in Baltimore?

9. Johnny Unitas had his best playoff game – based on quarterback rating – and added a rushing touchdown. Which current NFL team owner caught one of Unitas' two touchdown passes?

10. Who tied Raymond Berry for the team lead with five receptions?

1964 NFL Championship Game

The Colts' third NFL Championship game was a bit more disappointing than the first two. The team traveled to frigid Cleveland for the December 27 game. The Colts entered with a 12-2 record, but the Browns clearly dominated the game. Playing in their eighth championship game in 15 years, the Browns were led by quarterback Frank Ryan (206 yards and three touchdowns passing) and fullback Jim Brown (114 yards rushing). The game was scoreless in the first half, but Cleveland came on strong in the third quarter, scoring 17 unanswered points en route to their 27-0 win.

There has been no joy in Cleveland since. This is the city's most recent championship in any major professional sport. The Browns, Indians and Cavaliers have all drawn blanks in postseason play since 1959.

1964 Trivia

11. Which Browns receiver caught three touchdown passes to win game MVP honors?

12. The Colts rushed for just 92 yards in the game. Which Hall of Famer led the Colts in rushing?

13. Which Colts linebacker had the only interception off Browns quarterback Frank Ryan?

14. Who was the Browns kicker, known as "The Toe," who booted two field goals and three PATs?

15. Defensive end Gino Marchetti was named All Pro for the tenth time in 1964. Name any of the other five defensive linemen who played in the game for the Colts.

Super Bowl III

The Colts were 18-point favorites going into Super Bowl III, but that didn't keep Joe Namath from brashly predicting that his Jets would become the first team from the upstart AFL to win a Super Bowl. The Colts were 13-1 during the 1969 season and had blown out their opponents in the two playoff games leading up to the Super Bowl. The Jets' AFL was generally regarded as having lesser talent than the Colts' NFL, and many Jets were upset by the large point spread.

On paper, it seemed the Colts would win easily, but as it turned out, Broadway Joe was right. New York dominated from the outset. Colts quarterback Earl Morrall was intercepted three times in the first half, and the Jets were up 16-0 before the Colts scored late in the game.

Super Bowl III Trivia

16. Where was Super Bowl III played?

17. Which team did the Colts beat 34-0 in the NFL championship game to reach the Super Bowl?

18. Who scored the Colts' lone touchdown in the fourth quarter, when they were already trailing 16-0?

19. Earl Morrall and Johnny Unitas combined to

throw for more yards than Joe Namath. True or False?

20. The lone bright spot in the Colts offense was the back who rushed for 116 yards on 11 carries. Who was he?

Super Bowl V

The Colts had another chance two years later. Baltimore was back in the Super Bowl January 17, 1971, this time representing the AFC. Colts rookie Jim O'Brien kicked a 32-yard field goal with five seconds remaining to give the Colts a 16-13 win.

The game had 11 turnovers – a Super Bowl record – and Dallas had 10 penalties – another Super Bowl record – leading many to call this game the Blunder Bowl. Despite the victory, it was not a stellar day for any Colts player. In fact, the game MVP was a Cowboy, linebacker Chuck Howley. (It remains the only time a member of the losing team has won MVP honors.) Johnny Unitas completed just three of nine passes, with two interceptions. Earl Morrall was seven of 15, while running back Norm Bulaich had just 28 yards on the ground in 18 carries. Hall of Fame tight end John Mackey caught just two passes. Still, a win is a win, and it remains the only Super Bowl championship in Baltimore Colts history.

Super Bowl V Trivia

21. Where was the game played?

22. Which team did the Colts beat 27-17 in the AFC

Championship game to reach the Super Bowl?

23. Who had the interception that set up the game-tying touchdown in the fourth quarter?

24. Who had the interception that set up the game-winning field goal?

25. Why was Colts kicker Jim O'Brien nicknamed "Lassie"?

Super Bowl XLI

The people of Indianapolis thought it was a dream come true when their Colts made it to the Super Bowl. But when the game began in a driving rain and the Bears returned the opening kickoff for a touchdown, it started to feel more like a nightmare.

The weather conditions led to bad snaps, dropped passes and fumbles, but the Colts managed a 16-14 half-time lead. The Colts defense – much maligned throughout the 2006 season – took over in the second half, allowing the Bears just three second-half points. Quarterback Peyton Manning was named the game's MVP after completing 25 of 38 passes for 247 yards and a touchdown.

Super Bowl XLI Trivia

26. Where was the game played?

27. Which team did the Colts beat 38-34 in the AFC Championship game to reach the Super Bowl?

28. Who was the Super Bowl halftime performer?

29. What was the NFL's official slogan of Super Bowl XLI?

30. Which company was commissioned to make the Vince Lombardi Trophy at a cost of $25,000?

31. Nielsen Media Research reported 93 million viewers for Super Bowl XLI. How does this rate in Super Bowl history?

32. Who was favored to win Super Bowl XLI by Las Vegas odds makers?

33. Who sang the national anthem?

34. What were the weather conditions on game day?

35. The weather conditions led to a Super Bowl record – the most turnovers in one quarter. How many total turnovers were there in the first quarter of Super Bowl XLI?

36. Which player ran back the opening kickoff 92 yards for a touchdown?

37. Which Colts player caught 10 passes to set a Super Bowl record for running backs?

38. What was the score at halftime?

39. The Colts were the first dome team to win an outdoor Super Bowl. True or False?

40. One Colts player has been in five Super Bowls. Who is he?

41. During the Colts' Super Bowl victory parade, was the temperature in Indianapolis above or below 15 degrees?

42. How did the Colts score their first touchdown?

43. How many interceptions did Peyton Manning throw?

44. Who led the Colts in receiving yards?

45. Who was the Colts leading rusher?

46. Which former Indiana Mr. Football led the Chicago Bears to Super Bowl XLI?

47. Which defensive player missed all but four games in the regular season, but played in the Super Bowl and grabbed a key fourth-quarter interception?

48. What role did brothers Carl and Perry Paganelli play in the game?

49. Which Colts defensive back returned an interception 56 yards for the Colts' final touchdown in the game?

50. Who presented the Vince Lombardi Trophy to the Colts?

Answers on pages 103-106

Super Bowl XLI

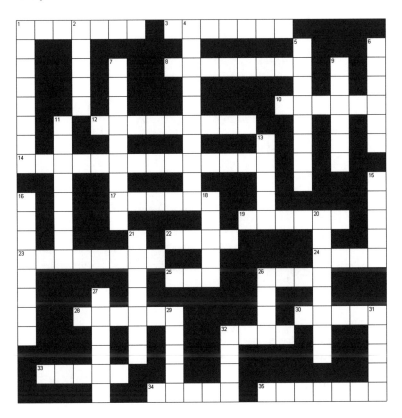

ACROSS

1. Game MVP
3. This Bears unit of Ayanbadejo, Gould and Hester was considered to be the best in the league: ____ Teams.
8. Bears quarterback
10. This Bears running back scored 6 touchdowns during the 2006 season.
12. These brothers were the first to officiate a Super Bowl game together.
14. Site of Super Bowl XLI

17. Colts' opponents in the second round of the AFC playoffs
19. NFL Today cohost with Brown, Esiason and Marino
22. The Colts are the first ____ team to win an outdoor Super Bowl.
23. Colts player with 12 touchdowns during the 2006 season
24. Giants running back who retired after the 2006 season

25. Network that broadcast Super Bowl XLI
26. Number of Super Bowl rings won by the Colts kicker
28. Colts' opponents in the first round of the AFC playoffs
30. Bears Pro Bowl kicker
32. First singer to perform the national anthem before two different Super Bowls
33. Bears running back who rushed for 1210 yards during the 2006 season
34. Scored the first Colts touchdown in Super Bowl XLI.
35. One of the Colts star pass-rushing defensive ends who had a key play in Super Bowl XLI

DOWN

1. This Bears receiver had 60 receptions during the 2006 season.
2. Play-by-play announcer of Super Bowl XLI
4. Ironically, Prince sang this song at halftime as it was pouring.
5. Bears defensive player who led the team with 12 sacks
6. Bears' opponents in the NFC Championship game

7. Colts kicker
9. Scored the first Bears touchdown in Super Bowl XLI (off the kickoff).
11. Bears starting linebacker and Pro Bowler
13. Bears coach
15. Colts rookie running back who led the team with 1081 yards and 4.8 yards per carry during the 2006 season
16. Bears' opponents in the first round of the NFC playoffs
18. Color commentator of Super Bowl XLI
20. Colts' opponents in the AFC Championship game
21. Super Bowl XLI was the first Super Bowl for this NFL Commissioner.
26. Number of Super Bowls played in by the Colts kicker
27. This Colts player rushed for 113 yards and a touchdown during Super Bowl XLI.
29. Presented the Vince Lombardi Trophy to the Colts.
31. First African-American coach to win a Super Bowl
32. Colts linebacker who led the team with 92 tackles

Answers on page 106

Chapter 3
2006 Team

Expectations were high for the 2006 Indianapolis Colts. After winning 13 consecutive games in 2005, they had a disappointingly short playoff run, so fans were hoping this might be "the year." The Colts started strong, winning nine straight games. But the team fell to Dallas in November, starting a 3-4 slide. The naysayers came out in droves, saying Peyton Manning would never win the big one, and that Tony Dungy was too soft to win a Super Bowl. The naysayers were wrong. In the postseason, the Colts shut down the Kansas City Chiefs, 23-8, finished off the Baltimore Ravens on the road, 15-6, and overcame an 18-point deficit to beat New England, 38-34, to make it to Super Bowl XLI. Safety Bob Sanders, who missed most of the season, returned to reignite the Colts defense.

The Colts' success was the result of stellar team play, but several individuals took top NFL honors, playing in the Pro Bowl. Five Colts offensive players – Tarik Glenn, Marvin Harrison, Peyton Manning, Jeff Saturday and Reggie Wayne — capped off the best Indianapolis Colts season ever with a trip to Honolulu.

2006 Team Trivia

Match each of the players on the Super Bowl XLI active roster with the statement that is true about them.

Offense:

Joseph Addai, Dallas Clark, Ryan Diem, DeDe Dorsey, Dan Federkeil, Bryan Fletcher, Dylan Gandy, Tarik Glenn, Marvin Harrison, Charlie Johnson, Ryan Lilja, Peyton Manning, Aaron Moorehead, Ricky Proehl, Dominic Rhodes, Jeff Saturday, Jake Scott, Justin Snow, Jim Sorgi, John Standeford, Matt Ulrich, Ben Utecht, Adam Vinatieri, Reggie Wayne and Terrence Wilkins

1. Set Big Ten records for career pass receptions and yards at Purdue.

2. His cousin is Brad Daugherty, former star of the Cleveland Cavaliers.

3. Has appeared in 112 consecutive games for the Colts, none as a starter.

4. Has been the starting right tackle for five seasons.

5. His brother, Terrell, played for the San Diego Chargers.

6. Won the Mackey Award as the top college tight end as a junior at Iowa.

7. Offensive lineman from Idaho; wears uniform No. 73.

8. Lives in Broken Arrow, Okla.; attended Lindenwood University, where he was a small school All-American defensive back as a junior and an All-American running back as a senior.

9. All-Pro lineman who went back to Cal to complete his degree in social welfare.

10. Appeared on "Wheel of Fortune" during Super Bowl week in 1999 to raise money for children in Syracuse, N.Y.

11. Tight end's first two receptions with Colts went for touchdowns.

12. Team's top punt and kick-off returner.

13. Running back worked at Dallas Cowboys' training camp while attending Midwestern State.

14. Backup quarterback played in Music City Bowl with Wisconsin.

15. The 2006 season was the wide receiver's 17th in the NFL.

16. His foundation sponsors an annual high school football bonanza at the RCA Dome.

17. Center/guard from Texas Tech.

18. Lives in Alberta, Canada; attended the University of Calgary; had 13 career sacks as a college defensive lineman.

19. Tied the franchise record with four touchdowns in a 2006 game versus Philadelphia.

20. Backup left tackle from Oklahoma State.

21. Has four Super Bowl championship rings.

22. Backup lineman from Northwestern.

23. Former Miami Hurricane has exceeded 1,000 yards receiving in a season three times.

24. Had started 75 consecutive games until an injury sidelined him versus Tennessee in 2006.

25. Starting left guard from Kansas State.

Defense:

Antoine Bethea, Rocky Boiman, Gary Brackett, Raheem Brock, Jason David, Dwight Freeney, Gilbert Gardner, Matt Giordano, Tyjuan Hagler, Nick Harper, Kelvin Hayden, Marlin Jackson, Tim Jennings, Cato June, Freddy Keiaho, Dan Klecko, Ryan LaCasse, Robert Mathis, Anthony McFarland, Rob Morris, Keith O'Neil, Darrell Reid, Dexter Reid, T.J. Rushing, Bob Sanders, Bo Schobel, Hunter Smith and Josh Thomas

26. Rookie defensive end who came to the Colts in a 2006 trade with Baltimore.

27. Leading tackler on the 2006 squad.

28. Purdue linebacker who started 12 games in 2006.

29. Defensive line teammate of Dwight Freeney at Syracuse.

30. Backup defensive tackle from Minnesota who led the special teams with 17 solo tackles.

31. Starting middle linebacker from Rutgers.

32. Rookie defensive back from Georgia.

33. Has 15 career interceptions; wore uniform No. 25.

34. Starting cornerback who led the team with four interceptions as a rookie in 2004.

35. Cal safety who started one game in 2006.

36. Defensive lineman who is a second-generation Colt.

37. 2006 sacks leader.

38. Notre Dame grad who started one game at linebacker; played in all 2006 games.

39. Rookie defensive back from Howard.

40. Defensive back who won a championship ring with New England in Super Bowl XXXIX.

41. Linebacker's father played seven years in the NFL.

42. Rookie defensive back from Stanford who was probably destined to be a running back.

43. Completed a pass in the Colts' playoff game versus Kansas City.

44. Defensive tackle who led the team with three fumble recoveries in 2006.

45. Backup cornerback who was the Colts' first-round draft pick in 2005.

46. San Diego State linebacker whose name is officially Naivote Taulawakeiaho.

47. Known as Booger.

48. Defensive end who was the Colts' first-round pick in 2002.

49. Earned Eagle Scout status as a teenager in Idaho.

50. Defensive end who played two years with the Titans; claimed off waivers by the Colts in 2006.

51. Safety who missed 12 regular-season games due to injury in 2006, but starred in the play-offs.

52. Cornerback who was a standout wide receiver at Illinois before switching to the defensive secondary.

53. University of Cincinnati linebacker who had 11 tackles as a special teams player in 2006.

Answers on pages 107-108

Team 2006 Offense

```
J I M S O R G I P I M E O E H P V X K R
E N Y A W E I G G E R E S S V F D N S Z
X J F S R Q R T L J O S E P H A D D A I
Z A Z C N V E A X I D G D I S C J T E D
P K J M M I I J Z Y E A O P I H N A J Y
I E A U R D T N L I S K H F Q A B R P G
R S Y V S F A A H L O J R T M R S I K V
B C E T R T N E T A E D C E Y L H K R X
F O S V O G I M H F R Q I A D I X G A A
G T R U A N V N F E N R N D A E S L L I
A T O N O B M S S M R F I U Z J F E C J
J I D G I P A A Z N L O M S L O D N S V
L Y E Q N T D E N E O W O B O H C N A O
I Z D C U U A H T N O W D M R N A J L D
L T E R R E N C E W I L K I N S C M L V
N E D N J O H N S T A N D E F O R D A C
A A T H C E T U N E B K G R O N R O D P
Y A T N R I C K Y P R O E H L U P A P A
R Y A N D I E M B X H C I R L U T T A M
O H Y F T N W B F P R T W T U F U Y K Q
```

Aaron Moorehead	Dylan Gandy	Peyton Manning
Adam Vinatieri	Jake Scott	Reggie Wayne
Ben Utecht	Jeff Saturday	Ricky Proehl
Bryan Fletcher	Jim Sorgi	Ryan Diem
Charlie Johnson	John Standeford	Ryan Lilja
Dallas Clark	Joseph Addai	Tarik Glenn
Dan Federkeil	Justin Snow	Terrence Wilkins
DeDe Dorsey	Marvin Harrison	
Dominic Rhodes	Matt Ulrich	

Answers on page 109

Chapter 4
Quarterbacks

The Colts' Johnny Unitas was selected as the quarterback for the NFL's 75th Anniversary Team. Could Peyton Manning be a shoo-in for the league's 100th Anniversary Team? When it's all said and done, the Colts franchise could lay claim to the two best quarterbacks in NFL history. With such a tradition, one wonders what would have happened to John Elway (and the Colts) if he hadn't refused to sign with the Colts when selected in the 1983 draft.

Besides Unitas and Manning, some of the other top quarterbacks in franchise history are Bert Jones, Earl Morrall, Jim Harbaugh, Jack Trudeau and Jeff George.

Quarterback Trivia

1. Which former AAFC Baltimore Colt holds the NFL record for most years in the league, at 26?

2. Who was the Colts starting quarterback in the team's first season in Indianapolis?

3. Which 1988 Colts draft pick and starting quarterback was the only QB to start for eight different teams in the NFL?

4. Which Hall of Fame quarterback embarrassed the Colts by threatening to pursue a baseball career instead of joining the team?

5. Which former Purdue Boilermaker played for the Colts and broadcast their games on the radio?

6. Who is the only other Colts backup quarterback from the 1980s who played college football in Indiana?

7. Which Colts quarterback met Queen Elizabeth II at a White House dinner?

8. Who was the Colts starting quarterback prior to the team drafting Peyton Manning?

9. Which Colts quarterback achieved the NFL's highest-ever passer rating in a season?

10. Which Colts quarterback is No. 2 in NFL history in average yards per pass in a game?

11. Who was the last Colts quarterback before Peyton Manning to lead the AFC in passing yards in a season?

12. In 1968, which Colts quarterback led the NFL in touchdown passes?

13. The Colts have retired just one quarterback's uniform number. True or False?

14. Since Peyton Manning joined the team, name any of the other eight players who have thrown a pass in a Colts game.

15. Place these players in chronological order by their tenure as the usual Colts starting quarterback: Marty Domres, Jeff George, Jim Harbaugh, Bert Jones, Peyton Manning, Earl Morrall, Mike Pagel and Jack Trudeau.

16. Who was the Colts starting quarterback the season before Johnny Unitas' arrival?

17. Entering the 2007 season, rank these quarterbacks in career passing yards as a Colt: Jim Harbaugh, Bert Jones, Peyton Manning, Earl Morrall and Johnny Unitas.

18. Eric Dickerson is the only Colts player to throw an interception in his only pass attempt. True or False?

19. Who holds the Colts career record for most interceptions thrown?

20. Who holds the Colts season record for most interceptions thrown?

21. Besides Johnny Unitas, name one of the other two Colts who threw five interceptions in a game.

22. Who holds the Colts record for most pass attempts in a game?

23. After Peyton Manning (who holds the top nine spots), who completed the most passes in a season for the Colts?

24. Who is second to Peyton Manning for most Colts completions by a rookie in a season?

25. Peyton Manning tied the franchise record by completing 17 consecutive passes. Whose record did he tie?

26. Besides Peyton Manning, who is the only starting quarterback to complete more than 60 percent of his career passes with the Colts?

27. Who are the only two Colts quarterbacks to throw for more than 400 yards in a single regular-season game?

28. Who holds the Colts record for most passing yards in a game by a rookie?

29. Besides Peyton Manning, who are the only Colts to throw for five or more touchdowns in a game?

30. Who completed the longest pass in Colts history?

31. Who holds the Colts record with 202 consecutive passes without an interception?

32. Who are the only three Colts QBs to earn 100+ quarterback ratings in a season?

33. Who was the Colts quarterback who threw for 340 yards versus Green Bay in a 1997 game?

34. Match these Colts quarterbacks with their colleges:

Chris Chandler	Central Michigan
Jim Harbaugh	Illinois
Gary Hogeboom	LSU
David Humm	Massachusetts
Bert Jones	Michigan
Greg Landry	Michigan State
Don Majkowski	Nebraska
Earl Morrall	UCLA
Tom Ramsey	Virginia
Jack Trudeau	Washington

35. Who was the quarterback from the Arizona Cardinals the Colts signed as a free agent in 1999?

36. Which quarterback has rushed for the most yards in his Colts career?

37. Which Colts quarterback has rushed for the most yards in a season?

38. Who was the starting quarterback for the Colts from 1948-50, who went on to a Hall of Fame career with the New York Giants?

39. Since 1963, which Colts quarterback was sacked the most times in one season?

40. Who threw for the most yards against the Colts in one game?

41. Who has thrown for the most yards in his career against the Colts?

42. Which Colts quarterback was nicknamed "The Majik Man?"

Johnny Unitas

Quarterback Johnny Unitas was a three-time NFL MVP, played in 10 Pro Bowls – a Colts record – and ended his 18-year NFL career with league records for the most yards gained, completions and touchdown passes, along with a dozen other marks. Perhaps his most impressive record, that still stands, is his 47 consecutive games with a touchdown pass. Unitas, known for his crew cut and black high-top cleats, was enshrined in the Pro Football Hall of Fame in 1979.

Not bad considering he was cut by the NFL team that drafted him and had to be coerced into leaving his construction job in Pittsburgh to try out for the Colts.

Johnny Unitas Trivia

43. How many times was Johnny Unitas named the NFL's Most Valuable Player?

44. Johnny Unitas was born and raised in a state known for its love of football. Which state is it?

45. Unitas played football at the University of Louisville. Which other three schools were on his short list?

46. Johnny Unitas was 6-foot-1 and weighed just 145 pounds on his first day of practice at the University of Louisville. True or False?

47. Why did Johnny U. play numerous positions (safety, linebacker, quarterback, kick/punt returner) in college?

48. What was Johnny Unitas' role in Super Bowl III?

49. With which NFL team did Unitas end his career?

50. Johnny Unitas understood Bob Irsay's reason for moving the team from Baltimore and was a strong supporter of the Indianapolis Colts. True or False?

51. Which college football award is named for Johnny Unitas?

52. Which record, considered unbreakable, does Unitas hold?

53. Johnny Unitas played a coach in a popular football movie. What movie is it?

54. The *Philadelphia Daily News* made a big Johnny Unitas mistake in 2003. What was it?

55. What shoes were Johnny U.'s trademark?

Peyton Manning

Peyton Manning was born to be a quarterback. Son of legendary NFL quarterback Archie Manning, Peyton grew up watching the NFL, studying the game and perfecting his football skills. He had stellar high school and college careers, but on Draft Day 1998, many so-called NFL experts didn't think the Colts should use the first overall pick on Manning. They thought the Colts should select Ryan Leaf.

Today Manning is a Super Bowl MVP, a two-time NFL MVP and destined to be the most prolific passer in the history of the league. Ryan Leaf? He played for four different teams in four years before giving up an NFL career. Today he is the quarterback coach and golf coach at West Texas A&M.

Manning is known as much for his off-the-field study and preparations as he is for his keen athletic ability. His clean-cut appearance and good guy image have made Manning one of the most popular and market-able players in pro sports today.

Peyton Manning Trivia

56. Peyton Manning has started every game since he joined the NFL. True or False?

57. Which country music singer is one of Peyton Manning's best friends?

58. Manning led the Colts to a victory in his first regular-season NFL game. True or False?

59. What is Peyton's full name?

60. How many siblings does Peyton Manning have?

61. Where did Peyton propose to his wife, Ashley?

62. Tennessee won the national title a year after Peyton graduated. Who is the only other quarterback picked in the first round of the draft who then watched as his college won the national championship a year later?

63. Why does Peyton Manning often lick his fingers after a play or pass?

64. Manning was born two days after which Academy Award-winning actress?

65. Who was the musical guest when Peyton Manning hosted "Saturday Night Live"?

66. Peyton cut short his career at the University of Tennessee, opting for the NFL after his junior season. True or False?

67. To what prestigious honor society was Peyton elected in college?

68. Who won the Heisman Trophy Peyton's senior year?

69. The University of Tennessee retired Manning's jersey number. What number is that?

70. In what TV ad does Peyton say, "That guy's pretty good...if you like 6-5, 230-pound quarterbacks with a laser rocket arm..."?

71. In 2004, Peyton Manning set a league record for the most passing touchdowns in a single season, with 49. Whose record did he break?

72. Where does Peyton Manning rank on the NFL's all-time passer rating list?

73. Peyton Manning threw for more than 300 yards in Super Bowl XLI. True or False?

74. What injury did Peyton sustain in the 2006 AFC title game?

75. Which pro season was Manning in when his Colts won Super Bowl XLI?

76. Since Peyton Manning's arrival in 1998, he has started every game. Only one NFL quarterback has a longer current streak (entering the 2007 season). Who is he?

77. In 2006 the Colts had a 4,000-yard passer (Manning), a 1,000-yard rusher (Addai) and two 1,000-yard receivers (Harrison and Wayne). It was the sixth time the Colts had accomplished that. Which other two NFL teams matched that feat in 2006?

Answers on pages 110-115

Team 2006 Defense

```
S R E D N A S B O B R O B M O R R I S X
U K K Y B L S Y R E L G A H N A U J Y T
L I E N O H T I E K L E B O H C S O B I
D W W L Z N I O G N I H S U R J T W D M
I Q J G V Q A C F O E K K R N K B N A J
E Z Y R E I A D H O C E J E S G A V N E
R C H O R E N D R A G T R E B L I G K N
R R U B H R T H J O X P O F R N R Y L N
E I N E U A O N A X I F O A T L Y A E I
T D T R D R I C V Y R G F B D H L E C N
X I E T U L N E K W D C T M T C G R K G
E E R M R V E T K Y M E S T H L E I O S
D R S A V P B O M Y B G N D A X N B W A
F L M T I Q E G N W D O X H M M U O S D
H L I H M K T O K K N D I U Q G J W M U
L E T I H O H F R A H E E M B R O C K N
U R H S T T E K C A R B Y R A G T U N N
Y R Y A N L A C A S S E Z V F N A Z D Y
Q A X A N I C K H A R P E R F J C Q L S
E D I V A D N O S A J O S H T H O M A S
```

Anthony McFarland	Gary Brackett	Raheem Brock
Antoine Bethea	Gilbert Gardner	Rob Morris
Bo Schobel	Hunter Smith	Robert Mathis
Bob Sanders	Jason David	Rocky Boiman
Cato June	Josh Thomas	Ryan LaCasse
Dan Klecko	Keith ONeil	TJ Rushing
Darrell Reid	Kelvin Hayden	Tim Jennings
Dexter Reid	Marlin Jackson	Tyjuan Hagler
Dwight Freeney	Matt Giordano	
Freddy Keiaho	Nick Harper	

Answers on page 116

Chapter 5
Running Backs

Running back Edgerrin James said: "All my life has been about proving myself." And prove himself he did, at least as a Colt. James ranks as the franchise's all-time career rushing leader, with 9,226 yards from 1999-2005. That easily eclipses the other top backs who have played for the Colts. It surpasses Lydell Mitchell, Marshall Faulk, Eric Dickerson, Lenny Moore, Tom Matte, Alan Ameche, Randy McMillan, Curtis Dickey and the latest Colts sensation Joseph Addai.

The Colts have a history of big-name running backs. Dickerson and Moore are the two ex-Colts in the Pro Football Hall of Fame. Dickerson played in Indianapolis from 1987-91 and made the Pro Bowl twice as a Colt. He led the NFL in rushing in 1988. Moore was in Baltimore from 1956-67 and played in six Pro Bowls. He set NFL records (since broken) with touchdowns in 18 consecutive games and 11 consecutive via the rush. He retired as the franchise's career rushing leader, a record that stood until Lydell Mitchell eclipsed it 10 years later, and is now held by the laid-back James.

"My total goal in life is to have fun," James said. "I just want to be out and around, chillin'."

Running Back Trivia

1. Who tied the franchise record with four touch-downs in the first 19 minutes in a game versus Denver on Halloween night 1988?

2. Who holds the Colts record for most career rushing yards?

3. Who holds the Colts record for most rushing yards in a season?

4. Which four Colts rushed for 1,000+ yards as a rookie?

5. Who holds the Colts record with 219 rushing yards in a game?

6. Who holds the Colts record with 147 rushing yards in a playoff game?

7. The Colts record for the longest run from scrimmage is 80 yards. Is the record held by Tom Matte, Alan Ameche or Edgerrin James?

8. Which of these Colts running backs had three rushing touchdowns in his first game in the NFL: Marshall Faulk, Edgerrin James or Joseph Addai?

9. Who was the only Baltimore Colts player with 1,000+ rushing yards in a season?

10. Who holds the Colts record for most rushing yards in one game by a rookie?

11. Who was the Colts running back who set a then-NFL record in 1964 with 20 touchdowns that season?

12. Which Colts running back was the emergency quarterback in the controversial 1965 sudden-death playoff loss at Green Bay?

13. Who set the then-NFL record with 40 carries in a 1974 game?

14. In 1974, Lydell Mitchell led the NFL in receptions, setting a then-NFL record for catches by a running back. How many passes did he catch?

15. Which two former Colts running backs are among the NFL's top 10 all-time leading rushers?

16. Who threw a touchdown pass, caught a touchdown pass and then returned a kickoff for a touchdown with 1:18 remaining as the Colts beat New England, 34-27, on a Monday Night Football telecast in 1978?

17. Who led the Colts in rushing in their final season in Baltimore?

18. Name the two Colts running backs who each ran for 100+ yards in a 1985 game versus Buffalo.

19. Who was the first Colts player to win the NFL rushing title?

20. Name the running back who set the then-franchise record with 240 yards from scrimmage (77 yards rushing and 163 yards receiving) in a 1992 game.

21. Who set the NFL Pro Bowl record with 180 yards rushing in one game?

22. When Edgerrin James led the NFL in rushing in 1999, he was the first Colts rookie to do so. True or False?

23. Who led the Colts in rushing yards in 1993? (Hint: He was a rookie from Northeast Louisiana.)

24. Who has rushed for more career yards with the Colts: Peyton Manning or Roosevelt Leaks?

25. Who holds the Colts record for fewest rushing yards in a career (eight carries for -18 yards)?

26. Who had more career receptions with the Colts: Edgerrin James or Marshall Faulk?

27. When did the Colts set their franchise record with 2,695 yards rushing in a season? Was it 1973, 1983 or 1993?

28. Is James Mungro's middle name Olevia, Olondo or Dondrell?

29. Which running back did the Colts acquire in a 2002 trade with New Orleans, who has the same name as a more famous running back?

30. Who rushed for the most yards against the Colts in his career?

31. Who has rushed for the most yards against the Colts in one game?

32. What was Alan Ameche's animal nickname?

33. Name one of Alan Ameche's famous cousins.

34. What was one of Lenny Moore's nicknames?

Answers on pages 117-118

Number Nineteen

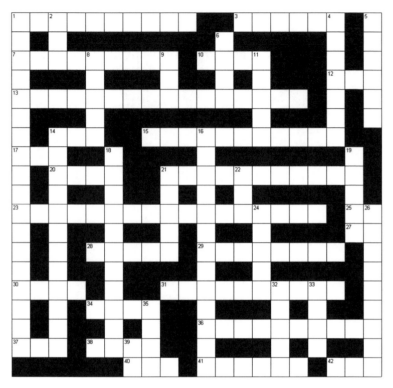

Questions about Johnny U. are marked with a .

ACROSS

1. Birthplace of Johnny 🄽
3. Johnny felt that this team was the true successor of the Baltimore Colts. 🄽
7. He threw a ____ pass in 47 consecutive games. 🄽
10. Not a win
12. Number of Johnny's Pro Bowl appearances 🄽

13. Team Johnny retired from 🄽
14. Happiness
15. Johnny's wife from 1972 until his death 🄽
17. Kanga's boy
20. Not there
21. Quarterback in Baltimore after Johnny 🄽
23. The Johnny Unitas Golden Arm Award is presented to the top _____. 🄽

25. Die from drugs (abbr.)
27. A drink with jam and break — or the seventh tone in a scale
28. Johnny was the first quarterback to throw for more than 40,000 _____. ∩
29. 1963 NFL MVP
30. Cut of meat
31. Quarterback in Baltimore before Johnny ∩
34. Johnny's first team: Bloomfield _____ ∩
36. Johnny's college ∩
37. Help (abbr.)
38. Pelt
40. The self
41. Johnny's coach in Baltimore ∩
42. Affirmative answer

DOWN

1. Team that originally drafted Johnny ∩
2. Nineteenth letter of the Greek alphabet
4. Johnny's number at the University of Louisville ∩
5. Enough
6. Wild hog
8. Covered with fuzz
9. Broadcast "The Greatest Game Ever Played" ∩
11. Where Johnny worked while playing as a Colt: Bethlehem _____ ∩
14. 1964 and 1967 NFL MVP ∩
16. Johnny's first wife and high school sweetheart ∩
18. Johnny's cause of death ∩
19. Assign as a portion
21. Exclamation of surprise
22. French sea
24. Groom's accomplice
26. Caught Johnny's first pass as a professional player ∩
32. Lazy, when found in a kitchen
33. Craving wildly
35. Music
39. In other words (abbr.)

Answers on page 119

Chapter 6
Receivers

What would Abbott do without Costello? Where would Ben be without Jerry? Can we even imagine Peyton Manning without Marvin Harrison? With big-name quarterbacks come big-name receivers. The Colts have had plenty.

The biggest name of all is Marvin Harrison. No. 88 holds the NFL record for most receptions in a season, is the Colts career reception leader and has grabbed 100+ passes in a season four times. Harrison is just the latest of the Colts stellar receivers. Raymond Berry was to Johnny U. what Harrison is to Manning. Berry (1955-67) retired as the NFL's all-time reception leader. The Hall of Famer was a member of the NFL's 75th Anniversary team. Complementing Berry was tight end John Mackey (1963-71), who was a member of the NFL's 50th Anniversary team and is also a Hall of Famer.

Receiver Trivia

1. Peyton Manning/Marvin Harrison is the most prolific quarterback/wide receiver touchdown duo in NFL history with 106. Whose record did they break?

2. Which Colts duo held that same record for more than 25 years?

3. Whose NFL record did Marvin Harrison break with 143 receptions in 2002?

4. Only three players in NFL history have more receptions than Marvin Harrison. Who are they?

5. What's the greatest number of passes Marvin Harrison has caught in one game?

6. Who was the Colts wide receiver selected to the 1980 All-NFL Rookie team?

7. Which Colts tight end was selected to the NFL's 50th Anniversary team?

8. Who retired in 1967 as the NFL's career reception leader?

9. Who is the Colts executive director of administration who had 411 catches as a Colts wide receiver?

10. Entering the 2007 season, who had caught more passes in his NFL career: Peyton Manning or Tarik Glenn?

11. Besides Marvin Harrison, who are the two Colts with 13+ catches in a game?

12. Who was the Colts leading wide receiver during the Super Bowl III season?

13. Who was the Colts leading wide receiver during the Super Bowl V season?

14. Who was the Colts leading receiver in Jeff George's rookie season of 1990?

15. Who was the leading receiver in Jim Harbaugh's first season with the Colts in 1994?

16. Who was the leading receiver in Peyton Manning's first season of 1998?

17. Who are the only three Colts with 200+ receiving yards in a regular season game?

18. How does ESPN's king of nicknames, Chris Berman, refer to Reggie Wayne?

19. Who had the longest touchdown reception in Colts history, a 90-yarder in 1975?

20. Among the Colts receivers with 100+ career catches, who has the highest average yards per catch?

21. Who holds the Colts record with 221 receiving yards in a playoff game?

22. Which Colts receiver is given credit for popularizing the use of wristbands and sunglasses in NFL games?

23. How many fumbles did Raymond Berry have in 13 seasons with the Colts?

24. For which NFL team was Raymond Berry the head coach?

25. Which wide receiver caught touchdown passes from seven different players in his Colts career, a franchise record?

26. Which tight end scored the final touchdown in Baltimore Colts history?

27. Which wide receiver did the Colts send to Atlanta as part of the deal that allowed the team to draft Jeff George?

28. Who set the then-franchise record in 1993 with receptions in 59 consecutive games?

29. In 2004, three Colts had 1,000+ receiving yards and 10+ touchdowns apiece. It was the first time in NFL history that three players from the same team exceeded those benchmarks. Who joined Marvin Harrison and Reggie Wayne on the list?

30. Who almost caught Jim Harbaugh's Hail Mary pass on the final play of the AFC Championship game at Pittsburgh?

31 Who holds the Colts record for most catches in a playoff game, with 12?

32. Who has caught the most passes in his career against the Colts?

33. Receivers Marvin Harrison and John Mackey both attended Syracuse and wore No. 88 for the Colts. True or False?

34. Which varsity sports did Dallas Clark play in high school?

35. Marcus Pollard did not play football in college. Where did he go to school, and what sport did he play?

36. Which team did Ken Dilger play for after the Colts?

37. Where was former Colts wide receiver Jerome Pathon born?

Answers on pages 120-122

Colts Hall of Famers

```
        O M B N B
      A B I A D H T P A W E
    L G R A Y M O N D B E R R Y A
  B O N C T M W R E K R A P M I J E L Z
K Q N L R N D F P O I D J U J M C G J I C O G F
P S V Q Y O L E O S K C I R D N E H D E T K G F J E M M
F N L S K N E M M N  O  V  P  M  I K C S W T Z W C R P
U V O E G R G K S O              C Z E Y P X L A F A B
F D R L V J P O C V  X  H  G  Y  K N A B W E B E E W H
  P D O N S H U L A H E R O O M Y N N E L V I S Z U O O Z
    N J U F F B N M F F G I N O M A R C H E T T I J
      E M A J O H N N Y U N I T A S Z C V O
        L C Y V W H E Q Z G Q S O F G
          L G P N O I Z Q I E N
              B B J D V
```

Art Donovan   Johnny Unitas

Don Shula   Lenny Moore

Eric Dickerson   Raymond Berry

Gino Marchetti   Ted Hendricks

Jim Parker   Weeb Ewbank

John Mackey

Answers on page 122

Chapter 7
Offensive Linemen

An NFL player said, "Let's face it, you have to have a slightly recessive gene that has a little something to do with the brain to go out on the football field and beat your head against other human being's on a daily basis." He must've been talking about the offensive line, the unglamorous group of men who are in the trenches protecting the quarterback and opening holes for the running backs.

The current linemen have excelled in both of those phases of the game. Center Jeff Saturday and tackle Tarik Glenn are the Pro Bowlers who anchor the line. Through the years, both in Baltimore (Bill Curry, George Kunz, Art Spinney, Dick Szymanski and Bob Vogel) and Indianapolis (Chris Hinton, Ray Donaldson, Will Wolford and Ron Solt), the Colts have had their share of recessive genes.

The best of the best was Hall of Famer Jim Parker (1957-67), who was named to both the modern all-time college team and the NFL's 75th Anniversary team.

Offensive Linemen Trivia

1. Who was the last offensive lineman the Colts took in the first round of the NFL draft?

2. Who was the guard from Maryland taken by the Colts in the first round in the 1984 draft?

3. I attended the University of North Carolina. I originally signed with Baltimore. I have started games at both center and guard. My name is a day of the week. Who am I?

4. Who was the All-Pro offensive lineman the Colts received as part of the John Elway trade?

5. Who was the two-time All-Pro center for the Colts who was the head coach at Georgia Tech, Alabama and Kentucky?

6. Who anchored the Colts offensive line from 1980-92 while wearing uniform No. 53?

7. Which guard, claimed off waivers by the Colts in 2004, was chosen First Team All-NFL by *Sports Illustrated* in 2005?

8. Which Colts lineman recovered a fumble for a touchdown in the AFC Championship game following the 2006 season?

9. George Kunz was a three-time Pro Bowl tackle for the Colts in the 1970s. Where did he attend college, winning a national championship?

10. Who was the Colts all-star center in 1960, known as Buzz?

11. Which Colts lineman was named to the NFL's 75th Anniversary team?

12. Who was the starting left tackle for the Colts in both Super Bowls III and V?

13. Which Colts guard made the NFL's All-Rookie team in 2004?

14. Which offensive tackle was the only Colts player named to the NFL's first All-Rookie Team in 1972?

15. Who is the Colts offensive line coach?

16. Which former Colts tackle is now a sports announcer for Indianapolis radio station WIBC?

17. Which Colts center became the Colts general manager in 1977?

18. Whose franchise record did Peyton Manning break for most consecutive games started?

19. Which current Colts lineman was the Illinois high school state champion in the shot put?

20. Jim Parker is the only Colts player to be voted All-Pro at two positions in the same season. True or False?

21. Which Colts guard shares a name with the 1972 Super Bowl MVP from the Dolphins?

Answers on page 123

Chapter 8
Defenders

They say that defense wins championships, and the Colts have been blessed with some top-flight defenders throughout their history. Dwight Freeney is just the latest.

Defensive end Gino Marchetti and defensive tackle Art Donovan led the Colts to back-to-back championships in 1958 and '59, and are both members of the Pro Football Hall of Fame. The two have been honored by the retirement of their jersey numbers. Another Hall of Famer is Ted Hendricks, whose stint as a Colt was short lived (five years) but productive. A three-time Colt Pro Bowler, Hendricks was a member of the Super Bowl V team.

Among the most intimidating players to line up on the Colts defense were Bubba Smith, Bobby Boyd, Mike Curtis, John Dutton, Gene Lipscomb, Andy Nelson, Bill Pellington, Bert Rechichar, Steve Stonebreaker and Rick Volk.

Along with Freeney, the recent defensive stalwarts include Duane Bickett, Cato June, Robert Mathis and Bob Sanders.

Defender Trivia

1. What World War II battle did Colts All-Pro defensive end Gino Marchetti fight?

2. Who was the Colts Hall of Fame linebacker born in Guatemala?

3. Who was the Colts first Pro Football Hall of Fame inductee?

4. Who holds the Colts record for career sacks?

5. Who was the Alabama defensive end the Colts selected as their No. 1 draft pick in 1986?

6. What is the name of Art Donovan's autobiography?

7. Who was the Nebraska linebacker the Colts selected with the fifth overall pick of the NFL draft in 1994?

8. Who is the Colts' career interceptions leader?

9. Art Donovan's father and grandfather were involved with a sport other than football. What sport is it?

10. Who holds the Colts record for most interceptions in a season, with 11?

11. Who was the last Colts player to intercept three passes in a game?

12. Whose name was on a fast food chain owned by several Colts players that eventually became Roy Rogers restaurants?

13. Which Colts player intercepted passes in five consecutive games in 1994?

14. Who set the Colts record with a 97-yard interception return in 1995?

15. Who set the NFL record for the longest return of an interception by a lineman, in 1992?

16. Name one of the two Colts players credited with six defensive fumble recoveries in a season.

17. Who was the last Colts player with two fumble recoveries in a game?

18. Who recorded a fumble recovery in three consecutive games in 1975?

19. Who holds the Colts record for longest fumble recovery return (95 yards) in a 2001 game?

20. What's the Colts team record for most passes intercepted in a game?

21. What's the Colts team record for most fumbles recovered in a game?

22. What's the Colts team record for most quarter-back sacks in a game?

23. What's Dwight Freeney's personal record for sacks in a game?

24. Who was the defensive back from Georgia the Colts selected in the second round of the 2006 NFL draft?

25. Who was the Colts defensive end named to the NFL's All-Rookie team in 2003?

26. Alex Agase, a Colts linebacker in 1953, was the head coach at which two Big Ten schools?

27. Which Colts linebacker was the NFL's Defensive Rookie of the Year in 1983?

28. Who was the NFL Linebacker of the Year in 1974?

29. Name one of the two Colts who tied for the NFL lead with seven interceptions in 1959.

30. How many yards rushing (on eight carries) did Walter Payton have his rookie season against the Colts?

31. Which two defenders did Don Shula name as player-coaches upon his arrival as head coach in 1963?

32. Who were the two defenders the Colts took with the first two overall picks of the 1992 draft?

33. Which Colts defensive back was the MVP of the 1957 Pro Bowl?

34. Which Colts defensive back recovered the Jerome Bettis fumble in the final minute of the recent playoff loss to the Steelers, only to be tripped up by quarterback Ben Roethlisberger?

35. Is the Colts record for fewest net yards allowed in a game above or below 50?

36. Who was the former Philadelphia Eagles free agent defensive tackle the Colts signed in 2005?

37. Which Colts linebacker walked on to his team at Rutgers and signed with the Colts as an undrafted free agent?

38. Bob Sanders changed his given name becauses it was difficult to pronounce. What is that name?

39. Duane Bickett was the NFL Rookie of the Year in 1982. True or False?

40. Which other NFL defensive star was Bubba Smith's costar in the short-lived television series "Blue Thunder"?

41. Which soft drink company hired Colts All-Pro defensive end Ordell Braase to appear (and even sing) in their commercials?

42. Which former Colts defensive tackle was a three-time Pro Bowl selection playing for the Pittsburgh Steelers when he died of an apparent drug overdose in 1963?

43. Which defensive tackle from 1990-96 known as Goose is now co-host of the DIY Network's "Man Caves"?

Answers on pages 124-126

Important Numbers

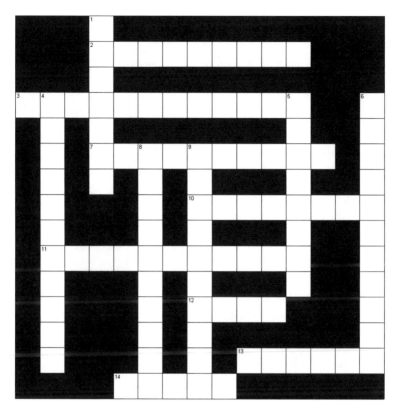

ACROSS

2. Ben Utecht and Bill Brooks
3. Jim Parker
7. Eric Dickerson and Joseph Addai
10. Peyton Manning
11. Ted Hendricks
12. Jim Harbaugh and Adam Vinatieri
13. Quarterback who wore 11
14. Number 82

DOWN

1. Art Donovan
4. John Mackey and Marvin Harrison
5. Johnny Unitas
6. Chris Hinton
8. Gino Marchetti
9. Lenny Moore

Answers on page 126

Chapter 9
Special Teams

Jim O'Brien's winning kick in Super Bowl V may be the most memorable special teams play in Colts history. But several other kickers have had memorable performances as well. However, in the world of NFL kickers, it's what have you done for me lately.

Take the case of Colts kicker Mike Vanderjagt. He went the entire 2003 season without missing a field goal and is the NFL's most accurate field goal kicker ever. But a missed 46-yard field goal in the final seconds of a 2005 playoff game at Pittsburgh led to Vanderjagt's dismissal.

The list of other successful Colts kickers includes Dean Biassucci, Lou Michaels, Toni Linhart, Cary Blanchard, Steve Myhra, Bert Rechichar and current kicker Adam Vinatieri.

Among Colts punters, the most proficient have included Rohn Stark, David Lee, Chris Gardocki, Tom Gilburg and current punter Hunter Smith.

Other key members of the special teams are the kick returners. The Colts have been blessed with some "special" ones throughout the years. Who can forget Clarence Verdin and his "Verdance," or Aaron Bailey, Albert Bentley, Bruce Laird, Terrence Wilkins, Troy Walters, Carl Taseff, Howard Stevens, Alvin Haymond, Rick Volk and Nesby Glasgow?

Special Teams Trivia

1. Who holds the Colts record for most field goals in a career?

2. Who kicked the Colts record 58-yard field goal in 1982?

3. Mike Vanderjagt did not miss a field goal in 2003. How many kicks did he make in the regular season?

4. Which two Colts kickers booted eight PATs in a game?

5. Who holds the Colts record for most punts in a career?

6. Colts punter Hunter Smith shares his name with a Colts staffer. What does the other Hunter Smith do?

7. Who holds the Colts career record for the highest punting yards average?

8. Who set the record in 1971 of 76 yards for the longest punt in Colts history?

9. Who returned the most punts in his Colts career?

10. Who returned the most kickoffs in his Colts career?

11. What's the Colts record for most punts in a game?

12. Who set the NFL record (that still stands) by averaging 23 yards per punt return during the 1950 season?

13. Who booted a then-NFL record 56-yard field goal in 1953, a record that stood for 17 years?

14. Who set the Colts record with a 90-yard punt return in a 1956 game?

15. Which Colts player was the first in the NFL with two 100+ yard kickoff returns in the same season?

16. Who was the first player credited with blocking a field goal attempt by jumping up at the crossbar? (Hint: He was also the first player to play out his option and change teams.)

17. Lou Michaels set the Colts record for kick-scoring points in a game. How many points did he score?

18. Which Colts player led the NFL in kickoff return average in 1968?

19. Which Colts player led the NFL in kickoff return average in 1972?

20. Who was the first Colts kicker to boot two 50+ field goals in the same game?

21. Which Colts special teams player appeared in the movie *Jerry Maguire*?

22. Which Colts kicker booted a 52-yard field goal in overtime to beat the Jets in 1995?

23. Who kicked four field goals in one quarter of a 1997 game to tie an NFL record?

24. Which Jets player returned a missed Colts field goal 104 yards to set an NFL record in 1998?

25. Who booted the game-winning field goal in the Colts' first regular-season overtime game in 1975?

26. Where did Colts kicker Adam Vinatieri attend college?

27. Who has been the Colts long snapper for the past seven years?

28. Which team has Adam Vinatieri kicked the most field goals against in his career?

29. Many believe Adam Vinatieri will be in the Pro Football Hall of Fame one day. Who is the only pure placekicker who has been en-shrined?

30. Which NFL postseason award did Colts kicker Jim Martin win in 1963?

31. Who returned a blocked punt for a touchdown with 20 seconds remaining in the game as the Colts beat Atlanta, 28-23, to avoid going 0-14 on the season?

32. Rohn Stark played in Super Bowl XXX. Which team did he play for?

33. Who booted the longest field goal against the Colts in history, a 60-yarder, in 2006?

34. Which two kickers filled in for Adam Vinatieri on extra points while he was injured for 3+ games in 2006?

35. What is the name of Hunter Smith's band?

36. Mike Vanderjagt was the kicking stand-in for which star of the Disney TV movie *The Garbage Picking Field Goal Kicking Philadelphia Phenomenon?*

37. Which Big Ten school did Mike Vanderjagt attend for one year as a reserve quarterback?

38. Which former Colts kicker is now an ESPN broadcaster of NFL games to Latin America?

Answers on pages 127-128

Peyton Manning

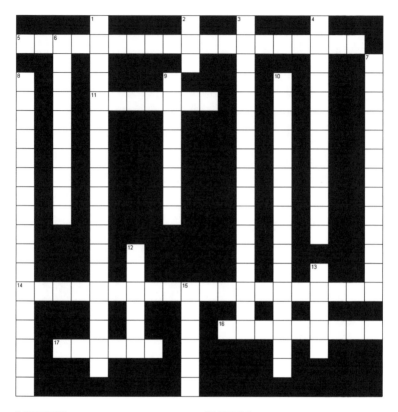

ACROSS

5. Peyton received this award for theoutstanding amateur athlete in the United States in 1997
11. The college his older brother attended
14. Peyton's major in college
16. Peyton's alma mater
17. Peyton's older brother

DOWN

1. Peyton's high school
2. Peyton's brother in the NFL
3. Peyton hosted this television show on his 31st birthday
4. Peyton received this award for the Nation's Top Player in 1997
6. Peyton does ads for this credit card
7. Peyton's brother is their quarterback

8. Peyton received this award for the Nation's Top Quarterback in 1997
9. Peyton's middle name
10. Peyton's dad was their quarterback
12. Peyton's dad

13. Peyton was the ___ pick in the 1998 NFL draft
15. Peyton passed this NFL legend's record for Most Passing Touchdown in a Single Season

Answers on page 129

Chapter 10
Drafts

Having high draft picks is both good news and bad news. Usually the top pick in the draft is reserved for the worst team in the league, whereas the Super Bowl champs pick last. The Colts have been at both the top and bottom of the draft order since moving to Indianapolis.

Among their No. 1 overall picks was Peyton Manning, who the Colts selected out of Tennessee in 1998. Their top picks have also included Steve Emtman, who played just three forgettable seasons in Indianapolis, and Jeff George, who became an NFL journeyman quarterback after playing four seasons with the Colts. One of the team's most memorable No. 1 selections – one many Colts fans would like to forget – was John Elway, who refused to sign with the Colts.

The draft has been reduced in size from 30 rounds in the 1950s to 20 rounds in the '60s to its current seven rounds. Yet the Colts rely on the draft to fill out its roster today as in previous years.

Colts President Bill Polian has shown his draft savvy with late-round picks that have contributed to the Colts' recent success. How important is the draft? Of last year's championship team, 28 players were acquired by the Colts via the draft.

Draft Trivia

1. Since taking Peyton Manning with the No. 1 pick in 1998, who is the only quarterback the Colts have drafted?

2. Who did the Colts draft with their No. 1 overall picks in 1953, 1967, 1983, 1990, 1992 and 1998?

3. Since 1982, who are the three running backs the Colts have taken in the first round?

4. Match these Colts draft picks with the round in which they were selected:

Raymond Berry	1
Eugene Daniel	2
Jeff Herrod	3
Cato June	4
Rex Kern	5
John Mackey	6
Robert Mathis	7
Lenny Moore	8
Jim O'Brien	9
Mike Pagel	10
Dominic Rhodes	20
Hunter Smith	Undrafted

5. Who was the last offensive lineman the Colts took in the first round?

6. Name the only two players drafted by the Colts in the first round who finished their college career at an Indiana school.

7. The Colts have selected three punters and kickers in the draft in the last 10 years. Who are they?

8. Match these Colts first-round picks with their college:

Duane Bickett	Alabama
Randy Burke	Brigham Young
Quentin Coryatt	California
Sean Dawkins	Florida
John Dutton	Kentucky
Steve Emtman	Maryland
Ellis Johnson	Nebraska
Barry Krauss	Southern California
Rob Morris	Texas A&M
Ron Solt	Washington

9. With their first-round pick in 2007, the Colts took Ohio State wide receiver Anthony Gonzalez. Name the four other Ohio State players the Colts have taken in the first round.

10. Since 1953, name the seven quarterbacks the Colts have taken in the first round.

11. Who did the Colts acquire in trades of their first-round picks in 1988 and 1991?

12. In the last 12 years, the Colts have taken two players from Syracuse in the first round. Who are they?

13. The Colts traded their 1996 first- and fourth-round picks to Tampa Bay for which quarterback?

14. When the Colts traded Eric Dickerson to the Raiders in 1992, they received fourth- and eighth-round picks. When the Colts signed Bill Polian as president in 1997, they had to give up a 1998 draft choice to the Carolina Panthers. Which round was it?

15. The Colts got a 1971 first-round pick when Coach Don Shula left for Miami. Who was the running back the Colts took with that pick?

16. The Colts received second- and fifth-round picks from the St. Louis Rams in 1999 for Marshall Faulk. Who did the Colts take with those picks?

17. Match these 2007 Colts draft picks to their college and position:

Anthony Gonzalez	Alabama State	Cornerback
Tony Ugoh	Arkansas	Cornerback
Daymeion Hughes	California	Defensive end
Quinn Pitcock	Ohio State	Defensive tackle
Brannon Condren	Ohio State	Outside linebacker
Clint Sessions	Ohio State	Offensive tackle
Roy Hall	Pittsburgh	Safety
Michael Coe	Texas Tech	Wide receiver
Keyunta Dawson	Troy State	Wide receiver

18. In which round of the 1955 draft was Johnny Unitas selected by the Pittsburgh Steelers?

Answers on pages 130-131

Chapter 11
Uniform Numbers

In 1973, the NFL began requiring certain positions to wear numbers within a certain range. For instance, running backs and defensive backs must wear a jersey number between 20 and 49. Players wear uniform numbers so viewers – fans, coaches, announcers and officials – can differentiate between players.

Through the years, the Colts have retired just seven jersey numbers. The franchise selected Johnny Unitas (No. 19), Buddy Young (No. 22), Lenny Moore (No. 24), Art Donovan (No. 70), Jim Parker (No. 77), Raymond Berry (No. 82) and Gino Marchetti (No. 89) for the honor.

Are players superstitious? Some are. No one in Baltimore Colts history wore No. 13. Since the team moved to Indianapolis, three players have dared to do so – Kelly Holcomb, Sean Salisbury and Mike Vanderjagt.

Sometimes players select their jersey numbers for sentimental reasons. Peyton Manning, who wore No. 16 in college, is now No. 18 – his father's old number.

1. Match these players with their uniform number:

Cary Blanchard	3
Ray Buchanan	14
Dallas Clark	28
Ryan Diem	34
Marshall Faulk	44
Cato June	59
Brad Scioli	67
Rohn Stark	71
Reggie Wayne	87
Will Wolford	99

2. Match these quarterbacks with their uniform number:

Jeff George	5
Mark Herrmann	7
Kelly Holcomb	9
Bert Jones	10
Blair Kiel	11
Earl Morrall	12
Mike Pagel	13
Jim Sorgi	15
Jack Trudeau	18
Johnny Unitas	19

3. Match these Colts, whose uniform numbers are
    retired, with their college alma mater:

Raymond Berry	Boston College
Art Donovan	Illinois
Gino Marchetti	Louisville
Lenny Moore	Ohio State
Jim Parker	Penn State
Johnny Unitas	San Francisco
Buddy Young	Southern Methodist

4. Name either Colts player who wore No. 1.

5. Which two numbers did Jim Harbaugh wear as
    a Colts QB?

6. Which two numbers did Dean Biasucci wear?

7. Which two numbers did Matt Bouza wear?

8. Who is the only Colts player to wear No. 70?

9. Who are the only two Colts players to wear
    No. 19 besides Johnny Unitas?

10. Who wore No. 18 with the Colts before Peyton
    Manning?

11. Which future Hall of Famer wore No. 25 for the Colts from 1953-56?

12. What number did tight end John Mackey wear during his Hall of Fame career?

13. Match these running backs with their uniform number:

Joseph Addai	20
Alan Ameche	23
Norm Bulaich	26
Eric Dickerson	29
Edgerrin James	29
Randy McMillan	32
Lydell Mitchell	32
James Mungro	33
Dominic Rhodes	35
Joe Washington	36

Answers on page 132

Chapter 12
Owners

The Irsays

Jim Irsay isn't your typical NFL owner. He hangs out with rock stars, plays in a band and could be described more as a hippie than a buttoned-up businessman. Yet the success of the Colts under his guidance is unmatched among NFL owners. Jim Irsay became the youngest NFL owner when his father, Robert Irsay, passed away in 1997. Jim was just 37 years old.

The elder Irsay, a Chicago businessman and self-made millionaire, obtained the Colts in a unique way. He originally owned the Los Angeles Rams and traded them straight up for the Colts in 1972. His tenure as Colts owner is best described as rocky. Baltimore fans considered him cantankerous and greedy. And that was before he moved their team in the middle of the night.

Irsay Trivia

1. Robert Irsay owned another NFL team before the Colts. Which team was it?

2. Which famous original coffee-stained manuscript does Jim Irsay own?

3. Where was Bob Irsay born?

4. Jim Irsay likes to call one of his favorite musicians "TP." Who is TP?

5. How did Robert Irsay die?

6. In what business did Bob Irsay earn his fortune?

7. Jim Irsay played himself in a movie directed by his friend Cameron Crowe. What movie is it?

8. Where did Jim Irsay go to college?

9. What was Jim Irsay's first job with the Colts?

10. Why did Bob Irsay move the Colts to Indianapolis?

11. Who was Bob Irsay's idol?

12. Which musical instrument does Jim Irsay play?

13. What tattoo does Jim Irsay have on his shoulder?

14. The *Chicago Tribune* ran an unusual photo of Jim Irsay. Why was it controversial?

Other Owners

The original Colts were owned by Bob Rodenberg and a small group of other investors. Within two years, the investors numbered in excess of 200. But in 1951, that franchise was dissolved and the city of Baltimore was without a team for two years. That's when colorful Carroll Rosenbloom headed the ownership group that brought football back to the city. In 1964, Rosenbloom bought out all the other minority owners to gain full control. A year after winning Super Bowl V, he traded the Colts to Robert Irsay in exchange for the Los Angeles Rams.

15. How did former Colts owner Carroll Rosenbloom die in 1979?

16. How much did the Colts ownership group receive from the NFL by withdrawing their franchise in 1951?

17. Which NFL commissioner awarded an NFL franchise to Baltimore and Carroll Rosenbloom in 1952?

18. How did Carroll Rosenbloom make his fortune, enabling him to purchase the Colts?

19. Who reportedly still has the Colts' original Lombardi Trophy from Super Bowl V?

20. Which Baltimore college's School of Arts and Sciences is named after former minority Colts owner Zanvyl Krieger?

Answers on pages 133-134

Colts Front Office and Coaching Staff

```
L V H J U T O M M O O R E D J B B L A D
L A D K V D S Q M W Z H C F P Z I C H G
V Z X D D U M D R A W O H D Q W L F Q Y
R X L Y R M R R O J Y T R M Y Y L T W V
J T R G P K W O F O G Z I N D L P A L D
X O B N N E X N A H W J S E E R O F J I
W M P U U I T M A N W S P W Y G L P O S
V T J D U I N E B T Q O O M T X I V N U
W E I Y W A U E M E W H L L D A A S T L
H L M N I J V K P E D G I K R N N L O E
R E C O R A T S R R T Y A D P A P L R W
H S A T O M K S A L E Z N O X D C E I S
J C L Y D E C H R I S T E N S E N N N A
Q O D E P S C J U N X N B L C R V R E O
U M W U E I F X N C T V C O A K T U Q Y
P J E H R R K V F K U U F P B A K P Z M
S O L E R S S A M O H T Y K C I R S E A
E T L N Y A A L A N W I L L I A M S J H
S J R E Y Y H P R U M E K I M F N U S D
R G N G G S P G V S Z P E T E W A R D B
```

Alan Williams	Jon Torine
Bill Polian	Mike Murphy
Bob Terpening	Pete Metzelaars
Carlos Woods	Pete Ward
Chris Polian	Richard Howell
Clyde Christensen	Ricky Thomas
Clyde Powers	Rod Perry
Gene Huey	Ron Meeks
Howard Mudd	Russ Purnell
James Irsay	Tom Moore
Jim Caldwell	Tom Telesco
John Teerlinck	Tony Dungy

Answers on page 135

Chapter 13
Coaches

The Colts history includes two Hall of Fame coaches and a good bet for a third. The winningest coach in NFL history, Don Shula, headed the Colts from 1963-69 and compiled a regular season record of 71-23-4. Weeb Ewbank, who hailed from Richmond, Indiana, led the Colts to two championships in 1958 and '59 and compiled a regular season record of 59-52-1 in his club-record nine seasons (1954-62) as head coach.

The team's first coach was Cecil Isbell, who also had an Indiana connection, having attended Purdue.

The Colts have had 20 head coaches, including Ted Marchibroda, who had two stints – one with the Baltimore Colts (1975-79) and another with the Indianapolis Colts (1992-95). But current coach Tony Dungy could turn out to be the most successful of them all.

Coach Trivia

1. Who was the head coach of the Colts when they moved from Baltimore to Indianapolis in 1984?

2. Who had the Colts just lost to when Jim Mora amused America with the quote, "Playoffs? Don't talk about playoffs. Are you kidding me? Playoffs? I just hope we can win a game, another game."

3. Which NFL Hall of Fame coach led the Colts when they lost Super Bowl III, the game in which Joe Namath guaranteed a victory?

4. Colts owner Carroll Rosenbloom hired Don Shula in 1963. Why was it a controversial move?

5. Weeb Ewbank became the Colts' second coach in 1954. Despite a record over .500 with the team, Ewbank may be disliked by Colts fans. Why?

6. Which "Ring of Honor" coach led Baltimore to three straight divisional titles in 1975, '76 and '77?

7. Which distinction does Frank Kush have in Colts history – most games lost in a season, most games won in a season or fewest games won in a season?

8. Which Colts coach had double-digit victory totals in each of his years with the Colts?

9. Which NFL team did Lindy Infante coach before the Colts?

10. Ron Meyer coached the Colts from 1986-91. Meyer was returning to his home state of Indiana, where he played college football. Which school did he attend?

11. At which two colleges was Rod Dowhower the head coach?

12. Who was the Colts' first coach, from 1947-48?

13. Which Colts coach played college football at Ohio State and won the Super Bowl in his first season with Baltimore?

14. Who is credited with recruiting Joe Namath to Alabama for Bear Bryant in 1961 before becoming the Colts coach?

15. Besides Frank Kush, which other coach led the Colts in Baltimore and Indianapolis?

16. In which two leagues did Ron Meyer coach after leaving the Colts?

17. Which two Colts coaches have sons who also were head coaches in the NFL?

18. Which Colts coach was the Occidental College roommate of NFL great and one-time presidential candidate Jack Kemp?

19. WhichColts assistant coach was promoted to head coach for the final 11 games of the 1991 season?

20. Which Colts assistant coach was promoted to head coach for the final game of the 1984 season?

Tony Dungy

Tony Dungy's .648 winning percentage in his first 11 seasons as an NFL head coach ranks No. 1 among all active head coaches. He also holds the distinction of winning a Super Bowl as both a player (Super Bowl XIII with the Pittsburgh Steelers) and as a head coach (Super Bowl XLI with the Colts).

The soft-spoken Michigan native worked his way through the ranks as an assistant coach at the University of Minnesota before moving to the NFL at Pittsburgh, Kansas City and Minnesota. His first head job was at Tampa Bay in 1996. Since Dungy took over the Colts in 2002, the team has posted double-digit victory totals and has been in the playoffs each season.

Dungy is well respected on and off the field. He is active in many charitable causes, especially in the Indianapolis community.

Tony Dungy Trivia

21. Tony Dungy played quarterback and coached at the University of Minnesota. Where did he first play professional football?

22. Tony Dungy is the sixth NFL coach to win 100 or more regular season games in his first 10 years as a head coach. Name one of the others.

23. Tony Dungy's .648 career winning percentage ranks him at what spot among active head coaches?

24. Which former Colts head coach's son was the offensive coordinator under Tony Dungy at the Tampa Bay Buccaneers?

25. Tony Dungy once threw an interception and intercepted a pass in the same game. True or False?

26. Tony Dungy is the only person in NFL history to win the Super Bowl as a player and head coach. True or False?

27. Tony Dungy is the first NFL coach to defeat all 32 NFL teams. True or False?

28. Tony Dungy's Colts are known for their great offense, but Dungy actually worked on the defensive side of the ball when he began coaching. True or False?

29. Which sport, other than football, did Tony Dungy play in college?

30. Which current NBA coach was a basketball teammate (and roommate) of Tony Dungy's at Minnesota?

31. What profession did Tony Dungy's parents share?

32. Where was Tony Dungy born?

33. Tony Dungy has the following traits according to his zodiac sun sign: diplomatic, urbane, romantic, charming, easygoing, sociable, idealistic and peaceable. What sign is he?

34. When Tony Dungy was 14 years old, he was featured in what national magazine?

35. Tony Dungy is a devout Christian and recently joined the Indiana Family Institute. During this association, Dungy has spoken out on what controversial issue?

Assistant Coaches

While the head coach of an NFL team gets all the glory – or takes all the criticism, depending on the team's success – there's a large group of behind the scenes assistant coaches who are even more tuned in to the Xs and Os of the game. There's an offensive coordinator, a defensive coordinator and several position coaches. While many are making their way up the coaching ranks, others such as Tom Moore, the Colts offensive coordinator, prefer the specialization being an assistant allows. Moore, for example, has become one of the pre-eminent NFL offensive specialists, having spent the last 30 years in that role with Pittsburgh and Detroit, as well as with the Colts.

36. Who was the Colts' assistant under Don Shula who became head coach of the Pittsburgh Steelers?

37. Who was the Colts' assistant under Don McCafferty who became head coach of the Denver Broncos?

38. Tom Zupancic was the Colts long-time strength coach. What is his current role with the franchise?

39. Which Colts assistant coach was the offensive coordinator at Tampa Bay under Tony Dungy?

40. Who is Peyton Manning's quarterbacks coach with the Colts?

41. Which current Colts assistant coach has the longest tenure with the team?

42. Who was the defensive backs coach for the 2006 championship season and the starting cornerback on the Chicago Bears Super Bowl XX team?

43. Who is the Colts' defensive coordinator?

44. Who is the Colts' offensive coordinator?

45. Which Colts assistant was a three-time Pro Bowl starter with San Francisco in the 1960s?

46. Who is the Colts' special teams coach?

Answers on pages 136-139

Answers

Chapter 1: History, pages 5-9

1. Charles Evans, who won a local contest.
2. The Dallas Texans franchise was relocated to Baltimore.
3. Green and silver.
4. 1953. The Dallas Texans franchise was moved to Baltimore and the Colts kept the Texans' team colors of blue and white.
5. The All-America Football Conference. The Colts played from 1947-49.
6. The Miami Seahawks, a franchise of the All-America Football Conference, that went bankrupt.
7. 1950, when the AAFC merged with the NFL.
8. Carroll Rosenbloom.
9. Fifteen.
10. 1954.
11. The Los Angeles Memorial Coliseum for a Colts versus Rams game in 1958.
12. 1957.
13. The Pittsburgh Steelers and Cleveland Browns.
14. A private plane crash-landed into Memorial Stadium's stands.
15. 1982.
16. Mayflower.

17. The strike-shortened 1982 season, when the Colts finished 0-8-1.
18. The Green Bay Packers.
19. Mike Pagel.
20. 1987.
21. The Tennessee Titans.
22. Robert Irsay.
23. Thirteen, in 2005.
24. Fourteen, in 1981.
25. The team scored 58 points versus Buffalo on Dec. 12, 1976.
26. In 1997, the Colts beat Miami, 41-0.
27. Marshall Faulk with 5,320 yards. Dickerson had 5,194.

    Bill Brooks with 411. John Mackey had 320.

    Bert Jones had 17,663 yards, while Trudeau threw for 9,647 yards.

    Eugene Daniel had 34 interceptions compared to Curtis' 21.

    Rohn Stark, with 985. Gardocki had 277.

    Marvin Harrison, who has 122 touchdowns. Lenny Moore had 113.

    Dean Biasucci, with 250 versus Blanchard's 105.

    Lou Michaels had 586, while James had 458.
28. Japan. The team lost to Atlanta, 27-21, in the Tokyo Dome.
29. Purdue's Ross-Ade Stadium. The Colts beat the New Orleans Saints, 17-0, on Aug. 12, 2000, in front of 20,105 fans.

30. The New England Patriots. The Colts were 89-39, while the Patriots were 83-45.

31. Polo Grounds, Yankee Stadium, Shea Stadium and Giants Stadium.

32. All of them except for Art Schlichter appeared in at least one Colts playoff game.

33. Bob Lamey.

34. The Colts beat San Diego, 34-31, on Dec. 26, 2004. Mike Vanderjagt kicked a 30-yard field goal 2:47 into overtime.

35. Lucas Oil Stadium.

36. Baltimore. It was against Pittsburgh, Nov. 13, 1983, during the team's final season in Baltimore.

37. Memorial Stadium.

Colts History, page 10

Chapter 2: Championships, pages 11-20

1958 NFL Championship Game

1. L.G. Dupre.
2. Steve Myhra.
3. Frank Gifford.
4. Ray Brown.
5. Raymond Berry.

1959 NFL Championship Game

6. John Sample, who had just one interception during the entire regular season.
7. PAT is an acronym for Point After Touchdown. His real name is George Allen Summerall.
8. Memorial Stadium.
9. Jerry Richardson, owner and founder of the Carolina Panthers.
10. Tight end Jim Mutscheller, who is from Beaver Falls, Pa., Joe Namath's hometown.

1964 NFL Championship Game

11. Gary Collins.
12. Lenny Moore, who had 40 yards on nine carries.
13. Don Shinnick.
14. Hall of Famer Lou Groza. The annual award presented to college football's best kicker is named after Groza.
15. Guy Reese, Fred Miller, Ordell Braase, Billy Ray Smith and John Diehl.

Super Bowl III

16. Miami's Orange Bowl.
17. The Cleveland Browns, the only team to beat the Colts in their 13-1 regular season.
18. Running back Jerry Hill scored on a one-yard run with 3:19 remaining.
19. False. Namath, the game's MVP, threw for 206 yards, while the Colts quarterbacks combined for 181 yards.
20. Tom Matte.

Super Bowl V

21. Miami's Orange Bowl.
22. The Oakland Raiders.
23. Rich Volk returned the interception 30 yards to the Cowboys' three-yard line. Earl Morrall called this the play of the game.
24. Linebacker Mike Curtis, who was considered one of the meanest players of his era.
25. Because of his long hair.

Super Bowl XLI

26. Miami Gardens' Dolphin Stadium.
27. The arch-rival New England Patriots. The Colts overcame an 18-point deficit for the biggest comeback in conference championship game history.
28. Prince.
29. "One Game, One Dream."
30. Tiffany & Co. of New York.

31. It was actually the third most-watched U.S. telecast ever, behind only Super Bowl XXX and the M*A*S*H finale.

32. The Colts were favored by seven points.

33. Billy Joel played the piano and sang. This was his second Super Bowl appearance, as he also performed at Super Bowl XXIII.

34. Miami was very rainy. In fact, it was the first time the Super Bowl was played in the rain.

35. Six. By the end of the game, the Bears had five turnovers and the Colts had three.

36. Rookie Devin Hester gave the Bears an early 7-0 lead.

37. Joseph Addai had 66 receiving yards and rushed for an additional 77 yards.

38. The Colts were ahead, 16-14.

39. True. The St. Louis Rams are a dome team, and they, too, won the Super Bowl. That was an indoor game, though.

40. Kicker Adam Vinatieri. His teams have won four of those games.

41. Below. Thousands of fans braved the 8-degree weather.

42. Reggie Wayne caught a 53-yard pass from Peyton Manning in the first quarter. (Adam Vinatieri missed the extra point.)

43. He threw one interception (in the first quarter) and one touchdown pass.

44. Running back Joseph Addai had more receiving yards (66) than Reggie Wayne (61) and Marvin Harrison (59).

45. Dominic Rhodes had 113 yards; his longest run was for 36 yards.

46. Quarterback Rex Grossman, from Bloomington South, who threw two interceptions in the game.

47. Safety Bob Sanders was hampered by a knee injury, but came on strong in the playoffs.

48. They were the first brothers to officiate a Super Bowl together.

49. Kelvin Hayden, who scored with 11:44 left in the game.

50. Former Colts player and coach Don Shula.

Super Bowl XLI, page 21

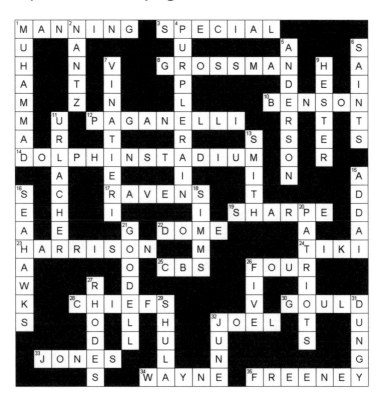

Chapter 3: 2006 Team, pages 24-29

Offense

1. John Standeford.
2. Aaron Moorehead.
3. Justin Snow.
4. Ryan Diem.
5. Bryan Fletcher.
6. Dallas Clark.
7. Jake Scott.
8. DeDe Dorsey.
9. Tarik Glenn.
10. Marvin Harrison.
11. Ben Utecht.
12. Terrence Wilkins.
13. Dominic Rhodes.
14. Jim Sorgi.
15. Ricky Proehl.
16. Peyton Manning.
17. Dylan Gandy.
18. Dan Federkeil.
19. Joseph Addai.
20. Charlie Johnson.
21. Adam Vinatieri.
22. Matt Ulrich.
23. Reggie Wayne.
24. Jeff Saturday.
25. Ryan Lilja.

Defense

26. Ryan LaCasse.
27. Cato June.
28. Gilbert Gardner.
29. Josh Thomas.
30. Darrell Reid.
31. Gary Brackett.
32. Tim Jennings.
33. Nick Harper.
34. Jason David.
35. Matt Giordano.
36. Dan Klecko.
37. Robert Mathis.
38. Rocky Boiman.
39. Antoine Bethea.
40. Dexter Reid.
41. Keith O'Neil.
42. T.J. Rushing.
43. Hunter Smith.
44. Raheem Brock.
45. Marlin Jackson.
46. Freddy Keiaho.
47. Anthony McFarland.
48. Dwight Freeney.
49. Rob Morris.
50. Bo Schobel.
51. Bob Sanders.
52. Kelvin Hayden.
53. Tyjuan Hagler.

Team 2006 Offense, page 30

```
J I M S O R G I P I M E O E H P V X K R
E N Y A W E I G G E R E S S V F D N S Z
X J F S R Q R T L J O S E P H A D D A I
Z A Z C N V E A X I D G D I S C J T E D
P K J M M I I J Z Y E A O P I H N A J Y
I E A U R D T N L I S K H F Q A B R P G
R S Y V S F A A H L O J R T M R S I K V
B C E T R T N E T A E D C E Y L H K R X
F O S V O G I M H F R Q I A D I X G A A
G T R U A N V N F E N R N D A E S L L I
A T O N O B M S S M R F I U Z J F E C J
J I D G I P A A Z N L O M S L O D N S V
L Y E Q N T D E N E O W O B O H C N A O
I Z D C U U A H T N O W D M R N A J L D
L T E R R E N C E W I L K I N S C M L V
N E D N J O H N S T A N D E F O R D A C
A A T H C E T U N E B K G R O N R O D P
Y A T N R I C K Y P R O E H L U P A P A
R Y A N D I E M B X H C I R L U T T A M
O H Y F T N W B F P R T W T U F U Y K Q
```

Chapter 4: Quarterbacks, pages 31-36

1. George Blanda, a place kicker and quarterback, played for the Colts in 1950.
2. Former Arizona State star Mike Pagel.
3. Chris Chandler, who played for Tampa, Phoenix, LA (Rams), Houston, Atlanta, Chicago and St. Louis, as well as the Colts.
4. John Elway, the Colts' No. 1 draft choice, refused to play for the team. He had a long and successful career with the Denver Broncos.
5. Mark Herrmann played for the Colts from 1983-84 and later joined the team's radio broadcasts for a stint as the color commentator.
6. Blair Kiel, who attended Notre Dame.
7. Peyton Manning attended a white-tie state dinner to honor the Queen in May 2007.
8. Jim Harbaugh, who played for the team from 1994-98. A "Ring of Honor" member, he moved on to the Baltimore Ravens when Manning came to town.
9. Peyton Manning had a rating of 121.1 in 2004 to lead the league. He passed No. 2 Steve Young (112.8) and No. 3 Joe Montana (112.4).
10. Johnny Unitas, who averaged 18.50 yards per pass versus Atlanta on Nov. 12, 1967. He completed 20 passes for 370 yards and fell just short of Sammy Baugh's record (18.58).
11. Jim Harbaugh, who threw for 2,575 yards in the 1995 season.
12. Earl Morrall had 26 touchdown passes that year.

13. True: It's the No. 19 jersey worn by Johnny Unitas.

14. Torrance Small, Steve Walsh, Ken Dilger, Mark Rypien, Brock Huard, Jim Sorgi, Jeff Saturday and Hunter Smith.

15. Earl Morrall, Marty Domres, Bert Jones, Mike Pagel, Jack Trudeau, Jeff George, Jim Harbaugh, Peyton Manning.

16. George Shaw.

17. Johnny Unitas, Peyton Manning, Bert Jones, Jim Harbaugh, Earl Morrall.

18. False. Zollie Toth holds this distinction. The running back's pass was intercepted in the 1954 season. Dickerson never threw a pass as a Colts player.

19. Johnny Unitas, who threw 246 in his Colts career.

20. Peyton Manning, who threw 28 in his rookie season (1998).

21. Fred Enke and Bill Troup.

22. Jeff George, who threw 59 passes at Washington, Nov. 7, 1993.

23. Jeff George, who completed 292 passes in 1991.

24. Jack Trudeau, who completed 204 passes in 1986.

25. Bert Jones.

26. Jim Harbaugh.

27. Johnny Unitas and Peyton Manning.

28. Jack Trudeau, who threw for 359 yards at the New York Jets on Nov. 16, 1986.

29. Gary Cuozzo and Gary Hogeboom.

30. Bert Jones threw a 90-yard pass versus the New York Jets in 1975.

31. Jeff George, who set the record in 1993.

32. Bert Jones, Jim Harbaugh and Peyton Manning.

33. Paul Justin.

34. Chris Chandler-Washington, Jim Harbaugh-Michigan, Gary Hogeboom-Central Michigan, David Humm-Nebraska, Bert Jones-LSU, Greg Landry-Massachusetts, Don Majkowski-Virginia, Earl Morrall-Michigan State, Tom Ramsey-UCLA, Jack Trudeau-Illinois.

35. Stoney Case, who never played a game for the Colts. But Case's high school team, the Odeassa Permian Panthers, went 16-0 under his guidance and was the inspiration for the book and movie *Friday Night Lights*.

36. Johnny Unitas, who had 1,777 yards.

37. Mike Pagel, who ran for 441 yards on 55 carries (8.2 average) in 1983.

38. Y.A. Tittle, who was a two-time NFL MVP.

39. Jeff George, who was sacked 56 times in 1991.

40. Joe Namath, who threw for 496 yards on Sept. 24, 1972.

41. Dan Marino, the Dolphins legend, who threw for 7,537 yards, nearly twice as many as runner up Jim Kelly.

42. Don Majkowski, who got the moniker in Green Bay in 1989. He played for the Colts from 1993-94.

Johnny Unitas, pages 37-38

43. Twice – in 1964 and 1967.

44. Pennsylvania. He was born in Pittsburgh in 1933.

45. Notre Dame and Indiana passed over Unitas. He was offered a scholarship to Pitt, but he failed the entrance exam.

46. True. Johnny's NFL playing weight was 195.

47. In 1952, the University of Louisville was deemphasizing sports. The college reduced its number of scholarships and implemented more stringent academic standards. Fifteen players lost their scholarships and they became a one-platoon football team.

48. Although he was sidelined with an elbow injury through most of the 1968 season, Johnny U. helped put together the Colts' only score, a touchdown late in the game. He did not play until the fourth quarter, but threw for more yards than the starter, Earl Morrall.

49. He was sold to the San Diego Chargers in 1973, and retired one year later.

50. False. Unitas tried to cut all his ties to the franchise and even asked the Pro Football Hall of Fame to remove his bust and records unless he was associated only with the Baltimore Colts.

51. The Johnny Unitas Golden Arm Award has been presented to the top senior college quarterback each year since 1987. The award is presented in Louisville. Peyton Manning won the award in 1997.

52. He set the NFL record for most consecutive games with a touchdown pass – 47 games.

53. He was in *Any Given Sunday* with Al Pacino,

Cameron Diaz and Jamie Foxx. Unitas played the head coach of a team called the Dallas Knights. (Bonus points if you also know he appeared in *Runaway Bride*. Unitas was an extra, sitting on a bench outside a bakery.)

54. The newspaper ran an article mentioning Johnny's 70th birthday. Unitas died in 2002. The newspaper ran a correction stating, "Johnny Unitas remains dead and did not celebrate his 70th birthday."

55. Black high-tops. Peyton Manning wore similar shoes in college and wanted to wear black high-tops to honor Johnny Unitas after his 2002 death, but the NFL would not allow it.

Peyton Manning, pages 39-42

56. True. He has started 144 games, the longest quarterback career-opening streak.

57. Kenny Chesney.

58. False. The Colts lost that game to the Miami Dolphins, 24-15.

59. Peyton Williams Manning.

60. He has two brothers, Cooper and Eli. Cooper is the oldest son, whose college career was cut short by spinal stenosis. Eli, Peyton's younger brother, plays quarterback for the New York Giants.

61. On the beach in Cancun, Mexico.

62. Vinny Testaverde of Miami.

63. Peyton says it has nothing to do with the game. It is just a bad habit that he has. He sometimes does it at dinner or when golfing.

64. Reese Witherspoon, who won an Oscar for her role in *Walk the Line,* was born March 22, 1976 – two days before Peyton.

65. Country music singer Carrie Underwood.

66. False, but Peyton did finish his B.A. degree (in speech communication) in three years.

67. He received Phi Beta Kappa honors and graduated with a 3.61 GPA.

68. Peyton finished second to the University of Michigan's Charles Woodson.

69. Tennessee retired Manning's number (No. 16) in 2005. He is only the third Volunteer player to have his number retired while still alive.

70. Sprint.

71. Dan Marino, former quarterback of the Miami Dolphins, held the record.

72. He is third, with a rating of 93.5, behind Steve Young (96.8) and Kurt Warner (94.1).

73. False. Peyton had 247 yards and one touchdown in the game.

74. A thumbnail bent all the way back.

75. It was in 2006, Peyton's ninth year in the NFL.

76. Brett Favre of the Green Bay Packers.

77. New Orleans and St. Louis.

Team 2006 Defense, page 43

```
S R E D N A S B O B R O B M O R R I S X
U K K Y B L S Y R E L G A H N A U J Y T
L I E N O H T I E K L E B O H C S O B I
D W W L Z N I O G N I H S U R J T W D M
I Q J G V Q A C F O E K K R N K B N A J
E Z Y R E I A D H O C E J E S G A V N E
R C H O R E N D R A G T R E B L I G K N
R R U B H R T H J O X P O F R N R Y L N
E I N E U A O N A X I F O A T L Y A E I
T D T R D R I C V Y R G F B D H L E C N
X I E T U L N E K W D C T M T C G R K G
E E R M R V E T K Y M E S T H L E I O S
D R S A V P B O M Y B G N D A X N B W A
F L M T I Q E G N W D O X H M M U O S D
H L I H M K T O K K N D I U Q G J W M U
L E T I H O H F R A H E E M B R O C K N
U R H S T T E K C A R B Y R A G T U N N
Y R Y A N L A C A S S E Z V F N A Z D Y
Q A X A N I C K H A R P E R F J C Q L S
E D I V A D N O S A J O S H T H O M A S
```

Chapter 5: Running Backs, pages 45-49

1. Eric Dickerson led the Colts to a 55-23 win on "Monday Night Football."
2. Edgerrin James, with 9,226 yards.
3. Edgerrin James, with 1,709 yards in 2000.
4. Marshall Faulk, Edgerrin James, Dominic Rhodes and Joseph Addai.
5. Edgerrin James set the record on Oct. 15, 2000.
6. Zack Crockett, who set the record at San Diego on Dec. 31, 1995.
7. Tom Matte, who had the touchdown run versus St. Louis on Oct. 12, 1964.
8. Marshall Faulk scored three times versus Houston on Sept. 4, 1994.
9. Lydell Mitchell, who had more than 1,000 yards in a season for three seasons.
10. Alan Ameche, who had 194 yards versus Chicago, Sept. 25, 1955.
11. Lenny Moore.
12. Tom Matte.
13. Lydell Mitchell.
14. He had 72 receptions that season.
15. Eric Dickerson and Marshall Faulk. Dickerson is No. 6 on the list, and Faulk is No. 9.
16. Joe Washington.
17. Curtis Dickey, who had 1,122 yards in 1983.
18. Randy McMillan, with 112 yards, and Albert Bentley, who ran for 100 yards.
19. Alan Ameche, with 961 yards in 1955.
20. Anthony Johnson.

21. Marshall Faulk did it in the 1995 game. He was the MVP.

22. False. Alan Ameche also led the league in his rookie season of 1955.

23. Roosevelt Potts.

24. Leaks. He was a running back and had 1,268 yards in his Colts career. Manning has 701 entering the 2007 season.

25. Punter David Lee.

26. Edgerrin James had 356 catches, while Faulk had 297.

27. It was the 1983 season, when the Colts were led by Curtis Dickey and Randy McMillan.

28. Olevia.

29. Ricky Williams.

30. Curtis Martin, who played against the Colts with New England and the New York Jets. He has rushed for 1,645 yards against the Colts.

31. Barry Sanders, with 216 yards at Detroit on Nov. 23, 1997.

32. The Horse.

33. Actors Don Ameche and Jim Ameche.

34. Lenny Moore had several nicknames, including Sputnik, The Reading Rocket, Lightning Lenny and Spats.

Number 19, page 50

```
P I T T S B U R G H  ■  R A V E N S  ■  P
I ■ A ■ ■ ■ ■ ■ ■ B ■ ■ ■ ■ ■ ■ I ■ L
T O U C H D O W N L O S S ■ ■ ■ X ■ E
T ■ A ■ ■ ■ B ■ A T ■ ■ ■ ■ ■ T E N
S A N D I E G O C H A R G E R S ■ E ■ T
B ■ R ■ ■ ■ ■ ■ ■ ■ E ■ ■ ■ E ■ Y
U J O Y ■ S A N D R A L E M O N ■
R O O ■ H ■ ■ O ■ ■ ■ ■ ■ ■ A
G H E R E ■ E A R L M O R R A L L
H N ■ A ■ G ■ O ■ E ■ ■ ■ L
S E N I O R Q U A R T E R B A C K O D
T Y ■ T ■ D ■ H ■ R ■ ■ ■ T I
E U Y A R D S ■ Y A T I T T L E ■ C
E N ■ T ■ ■ H ■ D ■ ■ ■ ■ K
L O I N ■ T ■ G E O R G E S H A W N
E T R A M S ■ E ■ ■ U V ■ Y
R A ■ C ■ O ■ L O U I S V I L L E
S O S S K I N ■ L ■ ■ A D R
■ ■ ■ E G O E W B A N K ■ Y E S
```

Across answers include: PITTSBURGH, RAVENS, TOUCHDOWN, LOSS, TEN, SAN DIEGO CHARGERS, JOY, SANDRA LEMON, HERE, EARL MORRALL, SENIOR QUARTERBACK, YARDS, Y A TITTLE, LOIN, GEORGE SHAW, RAMS, LOUISVILLE, SOS, SKIN, EGO, EWBANK, YES.

Chapter 6: Receivers, pages 52-57

1. Steve Young and Jerry Rice, who connected on 85 touchdowns in San Francisco from 1987-99.
2. Johnny Unitas and Raymond Berry combined for 63 from 1956-67.
3. Detroit's Herman Moore, who had 123 catches in 1995.
4. Jerry Rice (1,549), Cris Carter (1,101) and Tim Brown (1,094). Marvin entered the 2007 season with 1,022.
5. He had 14 catches twice – at Cleveland on Dec. 26, 1999 and versus Dallas on Nov. 17, 2002.
6. Ray Butler, who had 34 receptions for 574 yards that season.
7. John Mackey.
8. Raymond Berry, with 631 catches.
9. Bill Brooks.
10. They each have been officially credited with one pass reception.
11. Lydell Mitchell and Joe Washington.
12. John Mackey, with 45 catches.
13. Eddie Hinton, with 47 catches.
14. Running back Albert Bentley had 71 catches.
15. Floyd Turner and Marshall Faulk. Each had 52 catches.
16. Running back Marshall Faulk, with 86 catches.
17. Raymond Berry (224 at Washington in 1957), Roger Carr (210 at NY Jets in 1976) and Reggie Langhorne (203 at Washington in 1993).
18. He called him Reggie "Out of the Batcave" Wayne, in reference to Bruce Wayne (Batman).

19. Roger Carr, against the New York Jets on Nov. 16, 1975.

20. Jimmy Orr, who averaged 19.3 yards for his 303 catches.

21. Reggie Wayne, who set the mark versus Denver on Jan. 9, 2005.

22. Raymond Berry.

23. Two. (The wristbands must have worked.)

24. He was with the New England Patriots from 1984-89, where he went 48-39.

25. Glenn Doughty.

26. Pat Beach.

27. Andre Rison.

28. Jessie Hester.

29. Brandon Stokely.

30. Aaron Bailey.

31. Raymond Berry versus the New York Giants in 1958.

32. Andre Reed had 128 catches with the Buffalo Bills.

33. True.

34. Along with playing football, he was on the basketball, track and field and baseball teams at Twin River Valley High School in Livermore, Iowa.

35. He attended Bradley University and played basketball. Bradley did not have a football team when Pollard was in school.

36. The Tampa Bay Buccaneers, where he was a member of the Super Bowl XXXVII Championship squad.

37. He was born in Cape Town, South Africa, and was raised in Canada.

Colts Hall of Famers, page 58

```
          O M B N B
       A B I A D H T P A W E
     L G R A Y M O N D B E R R Y A
   B O N C T M W R E K R A P M I J E L Z
 K Q N L R N D F P O I D J U J M C G J I C O G F
P S V Q Y O L E O S K C I R D N E H D E T K G F J E M M
F N L S K N E M M N   O   V   P   M   I K C S W T Z W C R P
U V O E G R G K S O                   C Z E Y P X L A F A B
F D R L V J P O C V   X   H   G   Y   K N A B W E B E E W H
 P D O N S H U L A H E R O O M Y N N E L V I S Z U O O Z
   N J U F F B N M F F G I N O M A R C H E T T I J
     E M A J O H N N Y U N I T A S Z C V O
       L C Y V W H E Q Z G Q S O F G
         L G P N O I Z Q I E N
           B B J D V
```

Chapter 7: Offensive Linemen, pages 60-62

1. Tarik Glenn in 1997.
2. Ron Solt.
3. Jeff Saturday.
4. Chris Hinton, a six-time Colt Pro-Bowler.
5. Bill Curry.
6. Ray Donaldson, who played in Super Bowl XXX with the Dallas Cowboys.
7. Ryan Lilja.
8. Jeff Saturday.
9. Notre Dame, in 1966.
10. Madison Monroe "Buzz" Nutter.
11. Jim Parker, who won the Outland Trophy at Ohio State in 1956.
12. Bob Vogel.
13. Jake Scott.
14. Tom Drougas.
15. Howard Mudd, who has been an offensive line coach for 34 consecutive seasons in the NFL.
16. Joe Staysniak.
17. Dick Szymanski, who played 14 seasons with the Colts.
18. Ken Mendenhall, who started 115 consecutive games. He was a center from Oklahoma who played with the Colts from 1971-80.
19. Ryan Diem, who attended Glenbard North High School in Carol Stream, Ill. He was a four-time honor roll student.
20. True. He made the team as a guard and tackle in 1962.
21. Jake Scott.

Chapter 8: Defenders, pages 64-68

1. He fought in the Battle of the Bulge as a machine gunner after graduating from high school.
2. Ted Hendricks, a four-time Super Bowl winner (with the Colts and Raiders).
3. Art Donovan.
4. Dwight Freeney, with 56.5 sacks.
5. Jon Hand.
6. *Fatso*. It was published in 1987.
7. Trev Alberts, who is an announcer on ESPN. He won the Butkus Award as the nation's top college linebacker in 1993.
8. Bobby Boyd, who had 57 interceptions from 1960-68.
9. His father, Arthur Donovan, was a famed boxing referee, and his grandfather, Mike, was the world middleweight boxing champion in the 1870s.
10. Tom Keane, who did it in 1953.
11. Mike Prior versus Phoenix on Dec. 20, 1992.
12. Gino Marchetti's. Gino's Hamburgers, an East Coast chain with more than 300 restaurants, was owned by Marchetti, Alan Ameche and other players. It was sold to Marriott International in 1982.
13. Ray Buchanan, who is a Christian rap artist in his spare time.
14. Eugene Daniel.
15. Steve Emtman, who returned the interception 90 yards at Miami on Oct. 25.

16. Barney Poole (1953) and Stan White (1973).
17. Josh Mallard against Dallas on Nov. 17, 2002.
18. Fred Cook.
19. Chukie Nwokorie, who played at Purdue.
20. Seven. They did it against the Rams in 1954 and against the Bears in 1960.
21. Five versus the L.A. Rams in 1958.
22. Eleven versus the L.A. Rams in 1964 and versus the Cleveland Browns in 1992.
23. He has had three sacks on five occasions.
24. Tim Jennings.
25. Robert Mathis.
26. Northwestern and Purdue.
27. Vernon Maxwell, who recorded 11 sacks that season.
28. Mike Curtis.
29. Milt Davis and Don Shinnick.
30. Zero.
31. Gino Marchetti and Bill Pellington.
32. Defensive tackle Steve Emtman and linebacker Quentin Coryatt.
33. Bert Rechichar.
34. Nick Harper.
35. Below. Buffalo had just 49 yards on Oct. 10, 1971.
36. Corey Simon, who won a national championship at Florida State.
37. Gary Brackett. He won Defensive MVP honors his senior year.
38. Demond L. Sanders.

39. False. It was Chip Banks, who won the award as a Cleveland Brown. He ended his career with the Colts in 1992. Bickett was the NFL's Defensive Rookie of the Year in 1985 with the Colts.

40. Dick Butkus.

41. Dixie Cola.

42. Eugene Lipscomb, who played with the L.A. Rams for three years before joining the Colts.

43. Tony Siragusa.

Important Numbers, page 69

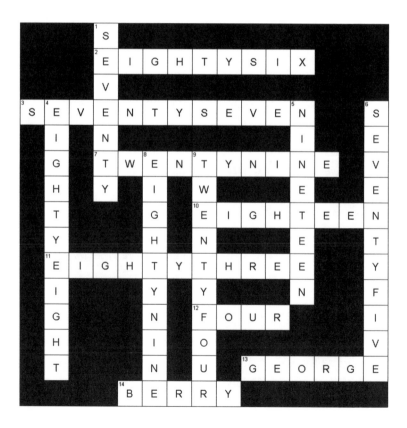

Chapter 9: Special Teams, pages 71-75

1. Mike Vanderjagt, who had 217 from 1998-05.
2. Dan Miller at San Diego on Dec. 26.
3. He connected on 37 field goals.
4. Tom Feamster (versus the L.A. Rams on Nov. 5, 1956) and Steve Myhra (versus Green Bay on Nov. 2, 1958).
5. Rohn Stark, who had 985 punts from 1982-94.
6. He is the head athletic trainer.
7. Chris Gardocki, at 44.8 yards per punt.
8. David Lee (versus the New York Giants on Oct. 17).
9. Clarence Verdin, with 156 from 1988-93.
10. Clarence Verdin, with 169 from 1988-93.
11. Twelve. Once by David Lee in 1977 and again by Chris Gardocki in 1996.
12. It was Herb Rich, who did it in his rookie season.
13. Bert Rechichar.
14. Carl Taseff.
15. In 1958, Lenny Lyles had 101- and 103-yard returns for touchdowns.
16. R.C. Owens.
17. He set the record with 18 in a 1966 game.
18. Preston Pearson, who played in five Super Bowls during his career with the Colts, Steelers and Cowboys.
19. Bruce Laird, who averaged 29.1 yards per return.
20. Dean Biasucci did it in 1988.

21. Dean Biasucci, who was with the Colts for ten seasons.

22. Mike Cofer.

23. Cary Blanchard.

24. Aaron Glenn.

25. Toni Linhart, who was a soccer player in Austria before moving to the United States.

26. South Dakota State.

27. Justin Snow.

28. He has 36 versus Miami. Vinatieri has met the Dolphins quite often in his career with the Patriots and Colts.

29. Jan Stenerud.

30. The Comeback Player of the Year Award.

31. Eugene Daniel in 1986.

32. The Pittsburgh Steelers.

33. Tennessee Titans' Rob Bironas.

34. Martin Gramatica and Hunter Smith.

35. He is part of an acoustic duo, Connersvine.

36. Tony Danza.

37. He went to Michigan State in 1988, before moving to Allan Hancock Community College in Santa Maria, Calif. He ended his college career at West Virginia.

38. Raul Allegre, who played in Baltimore and Indianapolis.

Peyton Manning, page 76

Chapter 10: Drafts, 79-82

1. Wisconsin's Jim Sorgi in the sixth round of the 2004 draft.
2. 1953 – Billy Vessels, 1967 – Bubba Smith, 1983 – John Elway, 1990 – Jeff George, 1992 – Steve Emtman, 1998 – Peyton Manning.
3. Marshall Faulk in 1994, Edgerrin James in 1999 and Joseph Addai in 2006.
4. Raymond Berry – 20, Eugene Daniel – 8, Jeff Herrod – 9, Cato June – 6, Rex Kern – 10, John Mackey – 2, Robert Mathis – 5, Lenny Moore – 1, Jim O'Brien – 3, Mike Pagel – 4, Dominic Rhodes – Undrafted, Hunter Smith – 7.
5. Tarik Glenn in 1997.
6. Halfback Marv Woodson of Indiana in 1964 and defensive tackle Ken Novak of Purdue in 1976.
7. Punter Hunter Smith (1999) and kickers David Kimball (2004) and Dave Rayner (2005).
8. Duane Bickett – Southern California, Randy Burke – Kentucky, Quentin Coryatt – Texas A&M, Sean Dawkins – California, John Dutton – Nebraska, Steve Emtman – Washington, Ellis Johnson – Florida, Barry Krauss – Alabama, Rob Morris – Brigham Young, Ron Solt – Maryland.
9. Jim Parker in 1957, Tom Matte in 1961, Bob Vogel in 1963 and Art Schlichter in 1982.
10. Cotton Davidson in 1954, George Shaw in 1955, Bert Jones in 1973, Art Schlichter in 1982, John Elway in 1982, Jeff George in 1990 and Peyton

Manning in 1998.

11. The Colts traded their 1988 pick for Eric Dickerson and their 1991 selection to Atlanta for the right to draft Jeff George.

12. Wide receiver Marvin Harrison in 1996 and defensive end Dwight Freeney in 2002.

13. Craig Erickson, who played just one season and completed just 50 passes for the Colts.

14. The third round.

15. Don McCauley.

16. Mike Peterson and Brad Scioli.

17. Anthony Gonzalez – Ohio State – Wide receiver, Tony Ugoh – Arkansas – Offensive tackle. Daymeion Hughes – California – Cornerback, Quinn Pitcock – Ohio State – Defensive tackle, Brannon Condren – Troy State – Safety, Clint Sessions – Pittsburgh Outside – linebacker, Roy Hall – Ohio State – Wide receiver, Michael Coe – Alabama State – Cornerback, Keyunta Dawson – Texas Tech – Defensive end.

18. He was selected in the ninth round, but was later released.

Chapter 11: Uniform Numbers, pages 84-86

1. Cary Blanchard – 14, Ray Buchanan – 34, Dallas Clark – 44, Ryan Diem – 71, Marshall Faulk – 28, Cato June – 59, Brad Scioli – 99, Rohn Stark – 3, Reggie Wayne – 87, Will Wolford – 67.

2. Jeff George – 11, Mark Herrmann – 9, Kelly Holcomb – 13, Bert Jones – 7, Blair Kiel – 5, Earl Morrall – 15, Mike Pagel – 18, Jim Sorgi – 12, Jack Trudeau – 10, Johnny Unitas – 19.

3. Raymond Berry – Southern Methodist, Art Donovan – Boston College, Gino Marchetti – San Francisco, Lenny Moore – Penn State, Jim Parker – Ohio State, Johnny Unitas – Louisville, Buddy Young – Illinois.

4. Matt Bryant and Dan Miller.

5. Nos. 4 and 12.

6. Nos. 4 and 5.

7. Nos. 85 and 87.

8. Art Donovan.

9. Cotton Davidson and Jack DelBello.

10. It was wide receiver Nate Jacquet in 1997.

11. Don Shula.

12. No. 88.

13. Joseph Addai – 29, Alan Ameche – 35, Norm Bulaich – 36, Eric Dickerson – 29, Edgerrin James – 32, Randy McMillan – 32, Lydell Mitchell – 26, James Mungro – 23, Dominic Rhodes – 33, Joe Washington – 20.

Chapter 12: Owners, pages 87-90

The Irsays

1. He acquired the Colts by trading the Los Angeles Rams to Carroll Rosenbloom in 1972.
2. He paid $2.5 million for *On the Road* by Jack Kerouac.
3. He was born in Chicago, Ill., on March 5, 1923, and attended the University of Illinois. (Jim Irsay was born in Lincolnwood, Ill., a Chicago suburb.)
4. Rock and Roll Hall of Famer Tom Petty.
5. He died of heart and kidney failure in January 1997.
6. Heating and ventilation. He joined his family's business in 1946, then founded the Robert Irsay Co. in 1951. It became one of the world's largest heating, air conditioning and ventilation companies.
7. *Jerry Maguire*, a 1996 movie starring Tom Cruise, Renee Zellweger and Cuba Gooding Jr.
8. He attended Southern Methodist University and has a degree in broadcast journalism.
9. He worked at the ticket counter and in public relations, beginning in 1982.
10. He said it was a fight with the city of Baltimore over Memorial Stadium that led him to Indianapolis on Mar. 29, 1984. Irsay wanted improvements, such as luxury boxes, or a new stadium.
11. John Wayne.
12. He plays the guitar, often taking it "on the road" when he travels with the team.

13. A horseshoe, in honor of the Colts.
14. He was naked, with just a guitar covering his private parts.

Other Owners

15. He died while swimming in the ocean. He was a skilled swimmer, so some people suspected foul play.
16. $50,000.
17. Bert Bell. Rosenbloom played football at the University of Pennsylvania under assistant coach Bell.
18. He was a successful businessman, known mainly for selling the U.S. Army its khaki uniforms during World War II.
19. Georgia Frontiere, owner of the St. Louis Rams, who was Carroll Rosenbloom's wife. The NFL commissioned a replacement trophy for the Colts, but it remains in the Maryland Sports Hall of Fame.
20. Johns Hopkins University. Krieger was a distiller, lawyer and entrepreneur, who gave $50 million to the school.

Colts 2006 Front Office and Coaching Staff, page 91

```
L V H J U T O M M O O R E D J B B L A D
L A D K V D S Q M W Z H C F P Z I C H G
V Z X D D U M D R A W O H D Q W L F Q Y
R X L Y R M R R O J Y T R M Y Y L T W V
J T R G P K W O F O G Z I N D L P A L D
X O B N N E X N A H W J S E E R O F J I
W M P U U I T M A N W S P W Y G L P O S
V T J D U I N E B T Q O O M T X I V N U
W E I Y W A U E M E W H L L D A A S T L
H L M N I J V K P E D G I K R N N L O E
R E C O R A T S R R T Y A D P A P L R W
H S A T O M K S A L E Z N O X D C E I S
J C L Y D E C H R I S T E N S E N N N A
Q O D E P S C J U N X N B L C R V R E O
U M W U E I F X N C T V C O A K T U Q Y
P J E H R R K V F K U U F P B A K P Z M
S O L E R S S A M O H T Y K C I R S E A
E T L N Y A A L A N W I L L I A M S J H
S J R E Y Y H P R U M E K I M F N U S D
R G N G G S P G V S Z P E T E W A R D B
```

Chapter 13: Coaches, pages 92-99

1. Frank Kush.
2. It was the 2001 season and the Colts had just lost to the San Francisco 49ers, 40-21, dropping them to 4-6.
3. Don Shula.
4. Some thought Shula, at only 33 years of age, was too young to coach in the NFL.
5. Ewbank was the coach of the New York Jets when they stunned the Colts, 16-7, in Super Bowl III.
6. Ted Marchibroda.
7. Fewest games won in a season. The Colts went 0-8-1 in the strike-shortened 1982 season.
8. Tony Dungy is 60-20 (regular season) in five years with the Colts.
9. He coached the Colts for two seasons after spending four seasons with Green Bay. His combined record with the two teams is 36-60 (.375).
10. He played defensive back at Purdue University.
11. Stanford and Vanderbilt.
12. Cecil Isbell.
13. Don McCafferty.
14. Howard Schnellenberger.
15. Ted Marchibroda was with the team in Baltimore from 1975-79 and in Indianapolis from 1992-95. He is now a Colts radio broadcaster.
16. The Canadian Football League (Las Vegas Posse in 1994) and the XFL (Chicago Enforcers in 2000).

17. Jim E. Mora's son, Jim L. Mora, was head coach of the Atlanta Falcons. Don Shula's son, Dave, coached the Cincinnati Bengals.
18. Jim Mora.
19. Rick Venturi.
20. Hal Hunter.

Tony Dungy

21. He joined the Pittsburgh Steelers in 1977. The team converted him from quarterback to wide receiver, and then to safety.
22. George Seifert, Don Shula, John Madden, Joe Gibbs and Mike Ditka.
23. Second, behind the Redskins' Joe Gibbs.
24. Don Shula's son, Mike, was with Tampa Bay from 1996-99.
25. True. Dungy, who typically played safety for the Steelers, was also an emergency backup quarterback. He threw and caught interceptions in a 1977 game versus the Colts.
26. False, but Mike Ditka and Tom Flores are the only others who have achieved this feat.
27. True.
28. True. Dungy was an assistant coach at the University of Minnesota before working with the NFL defenses in Pittsburgh, Minnesota and Kansas City.
29. As a freshman, he played for the Golden Gophers basketball team. He averaged 2.6 points per game in his only basketball season.
30. Detroit Pistons head coach Flip Saunders.

31. Teaching. His father was a college professor and his mother was a middle school teacher.

32. He is from Jackson, Mich., and graduated from Parkside High School.

33. Born Oct. 6, 1955, Dungy is a Libra.

34. *Sports Illustrated* ran his picture and a short bio in its "Faces in the Crowd" column.

35. Gay marriage. Dungy hopes to ban gay marriage in Indiana.

Assistant Coaches

36. Chuck Noll, who won four Super Bowls with the Steelers.

37. Red Miller, who took his team to Super Bowl XII.

38. He is the team's senior vice president of sales and marketing, but still ranks fourteenth in the world among all-time super heavyweights lifters.

39. Clyde Christensen, who now coaches the Colts wide receivers.

40. Jim Caldwell, the former Wake Forest head coach.

41. Running backs coach Gene Huey, who has been with the team for 16 years.

42. Leslie Frazier.

43. Ron Meeks, who is in his sixth year with the Colts and played five seasons in the Canadian Football League.

44. Tom Moore, who has been coaching for 44 years now.

45. Howard Mudd, who is in his 34th consecutive season as an offensive line coach, and his tenth with the Colts.

46. Russ Purnell, a 22-year NFL coaching veteran.

Sources:

For more information about the Indianapolis Colts, we encourage you to visit the following websites:

www.nfl.com

www.wikipedia.com

If you liked this book, you might also like:

California Crosswords
Dale Ratermann & H.W. Kondras

BR • $6.95 • 128 pgs • 5.5x8.5 • ISBN: 097633612X • TP

Illinois Crosswords
Dale Ratermann & H.W. Kondras

BR • $6.95 • 128 pgs • 5.5x8.5 • ISBN: 0971895988 • TP

Indiana Crosswords
H.W. Kondras

BR • $6.95 • 128 pgs • 5.5x8.5 • ISBN: 0971895929 • TP

Seek and Find Indiana
H.W. Kondras

BR • $5.95 • 160 pgs • 5.5x8.5 • ISBN: 0976336154 • TP

Florida Crosswords
Dale Ratermann & H.W. Kondras

BR • $6.95 • 160 pgs • 5.5x8.5 • ISBN: 0976336170 • TP

New York Crosswords
Dale Ratermann & H.W. Kondras

BR • $6.95 • 128 pgs • 5.5x8.5 • ISBN: 0976336103 • TP

Ohio Crosswords
Dale Ratermann & H.W. Kondras

BR • $6.95 • 128 pgs • 5.5x8.5 • ISBN: 097189597X • TP

Texas Crosswords
Dale Ratermann & H.W. Kondras

BR • $6.95 • 128 pgs • 5.5x8.5 • ISBN: 0971895996 • TP

Wisconsin Crosswords
Dale Ratermann & H.W. Kondras

BR • $6.95 • 128 pgs • 5.5x8.5 • ISBN: 0976336146 • TP